edited by
Jean Radford
Hatfield Polytechnic

The Progress of Romance
The Politics of Popular Fiction

First published in 1986 by
Routledge & Kegan Paul plc
11 New Fetter Lane, London EC4P 4EE

Published in the USA by
Routledge & Kegan Paul Inc.
in association with Methuen Inc.
29 West 35th Street, New York, NY 10001

Set in 11 on 13 pt Bembo
by Columns of Reading
and printed in Great Britain
by Billings & Sons Ltd, Worcester

Library of Congress Cataloging in Publication Data

The progress of romance
(History workshop series)
Contents: Introduction / Jean Radford — The Greek
romance / Margaret Williamson — The politics of
seduction in English popular culture, 1748–1848 / Anna
Clark — [etc.]
1. Love stories, English—History and criticism.
2. Love stories, American—History and criticism.
3. Popular literature—History and criticism.
4. Feminism and literature. 5. Women—Books and
reading. I. Radford, Jean. II. Series.
PR830.L69R4   1986   823'.085'09   86–6593
British Library CIP Data also available
ISBN 0-7102-0717-4 (c)
      0-7102-0963-0 (p)

Contents

Illustrations

Contributors

Christine Bridgwood is a research student at the University of Sussex working on a study of women, consumerism and popular culture in the late 1950s and early 1960s.

Anna Clark is an active member of the London Feminist History Group, and the author of a forthcoming work on sexual assault, 1770–1845.

Ann Rosalind Jones is Associate Professor of Comparative Literature at Smith College, Massachussetts. Her research interests include feminist literary theory and women's writing in the Renaissance and the twentieth century.

Alison Light is a Lecturer in English at Brighton Polytechnic. She is working on a study of British women's writing 1945–60.

Derrick Price teaches in the Faculty of Art and Design at Bristol Polytechnic. He is a member of Collective Design Projects and is working at the Birmingham Centre for Contemporary Cultural Studies on a study of representations of South Wales.

Jean Radford teaches English and American literature at Hatfield Polytechnic. She is the author of *Norman Mailer* and *Dorothy Richardson: A Woman's Writer* (forthcoming), and has written variously on feminism, psychoanalysis and cultural politics.

Michele Roberts writes poetry and short stories and is the author of three novels, *A Piece of the Night*, *The Visitation* and *The Wild Girl*.

Helen Taylor teaches at Bristol Polytechnic. She has published articles on women writers and co-authored an introduction to women's studies. Her doctoral research focused on Louisiana women's writing and she is currently preparing a book on *Gone With the Wind*.

Margaret Williamson has taught Classics and English in adult education institutes and in universities. She is currently writing a book on Sappho for Virago Press.

THE
PROGRESS of ROMANCE,

THROUGH
TIMES, COUNTRIES, AND MANNERS;

WITH

REMARKS
ON THE GOOD AND BAD EFFECTS OF
IT, ON THEM RESPECTIVELY;

IN A COURSE OF

EVENING CONVERSATIONS.

BY C. R. AUTHOR OF
THE ENGLISH BARON, THE TWO MENTORS, &c.

IN TWO VOLUMES.
VOL. I.

It hath bene through all ages ever feene,
That with the praife of armes and chevalrie
The prize of beautie ftill hath ioyned beene,
And that for reafons fpeciall privitee,
For either doth on other much relie :
For he me feemes moft fit the faire to ferve,
That can her beft defend from villenie,
And fhe moft fit his fervice doth deferve,
That faireft is, and from her faith will never fwerve.

SPENSER's Faery Queene. Book 4. Canto 5. Stanza 1.

PRINTED FOR THE AUTHOR,
BY W. KEYMER, COLCHESTER, AND SOLD BY HIM;
SOLD ALSO BY G. G. J. AND J. ROBINSON,
IN PATER-NOSTER ROW, LONDON.
MDCCLXXXV.

Title page from *The Progress of Romance* (1785) by Clara Reeve (British Library)

1
Introduction

JEAN RADFORD

This is a time of renewed interest in all forms of popular culture. The need to understand different sources of pleasure and identification, whether in popular fiction or political populism, has led to a fresh and creative engagement with 'the popular'. What are the ways in which people's hopes and dreams, fears and fantasies, are invested in what they read and watch? And what needs, real or imaginary, are created and satisfied in the process? Suddenly, these questions have assumed a new importance.

Since the emergence of new technologies and changed patterns of work and leisure after the Second World War, 'mass' culture has grown enormously. The last decade of recession and unemployment has strengthened rather than weakened this trend, while the interaction between elite and popular art forms, between written and televisual productions, is now marked even in the 'highest' of literary forms. Since the 1970s crisis in literary studies in higher education, it is less and less possible to ignore 90 per cent of what is written and read, and gradually syllabuses are changing – in schools as well as in polytechnics and universities. While commercial interests have monitored these developments with some care, the *political* effects of popular cultural activity are now receiving increasing attention from cultural radicals, feminists, and all those interested in the way meanings and values are produced and lived.

Is there a distinctive aesthetics of popular culture, or are the popular arts simply degraded and naive forms of the fine arts? John Cawelti, in his influential study of popular writing *Adventure, Mystery and Romance*,[1] traces this question back to Plato's argument about the powers of rhetoric in *The Republic*, while claiming that it is still the starting point for current debates. Does popular culture embody traditions of resistance to the dominant culture, or is it merely a means of domination and control? 'Containment or resistance?' asks Stuart Hall.[2] Might 'the romance-reading clubs and fanzines springing up across the States . . . be the seedbed of a new subversive women's art form', as one feminist reviewer suggested recently? Or is it rather, as an exasperated voice in the same journal claimed, that 'trash is trash is trash'?[3]

The aim of this collection is to present some of the new thinking on popular writing to a wider audience, but also to offer a historical perspective on a specific form of popular fiction: the romance. It is hoped that essays on other forms of popular writing – notably crime and science fiction – will follow. It is also hoped that our discussions will feed into the larger theoretical project called for by Tony Bennett, one which would 'focus on differences between forms of writing, explaining these with reference to the historically specific materials and ideological constraints which regulate their production'.[4] The emphasis of many of the contributions here is also on the *reproduction* of popular texts and the ideological constraints which regulate the ways in which readers can *use* those texts. This, as I argue later, we consider a crucial dimension in the analysis of popular culture.

Most of the essays here were originally presented at the first History Workshop Conference on Popular

Literature held at Ruskin College, Oxford, in May 1984. They reflect diverse positions and methods within the current debate: sociological, psychoanalytic and literary. Some focus more on texts or readers, others concentrate on theoretical questions about narrative or ideology. What they have in common is that each refuses the notion of popular writing as the contaminated spawn of industrialism, in favour of a historically specific understanding of popular forms and their uses.

Art and the popular

As with social history twenty years or so ago, there is much unexplored territory for cultural history which includes the popular. (Cultural histories of art or literature which *exclude* it have of course been the staple diet for students of 'the Humanities'.) The objective is not to displace traditional histories of high culture, by a parallel and oppositional history of what has been left out from these, but to re-define the relationship between elite and popular art forms as different social developments within the same field.

The term 'popular' is itself a notoriously unstable category, one which has not only undergone changes in meaning since its derivation from the Latin 'popularis' (belonging to the people), but which is in its present usage ambiguous, having accumulated a number of contradictory senses of both a positive and negative kind. As Raymond Williams points out, 'popular' may mean: of the people as opposed to their rulers; well-liked or widely read; inferior or base; that which presents new or specialised knowledge in an accessible way.[5] It can only be understood *in relation* to what it is being opposed to in a historically given instance; the popular or 'quality' press, popular or classical music, but also the *Popular* Front or a *popular* textbook. The categories high/low and popular/art are thus interdependent and shifting, so that what is being designated or distinguished changes from period to period according to a wider set of social practices and institutions. So, for example, what is popular in its own period may become Art in another, as Northrop Frye comments on literary history:

> Spenser has acquired a reputation as a poet's poet and a storehouse of recondite allusion and allegory; but in his day *The Faerie Queene* was regarded as pandering to a middlebrow appetite for stories about fearless knights and beauteous maidens and hideous ogres and dragons, instead of following more sober classical models.[6]

With this example, the popular text survives by becoming included in a literary establishment or 'canon', changing its significance in doing so. Frye argues, indeed, that this is the *only* way in which popular art of one period can survive into another – a judgement which ignores the broader cultural continuities which may maintain the 'popularity' of a non-canonical text like *Pilgrim's Progress*. His formalist[7] view also fails to take into account certain historical *dis*continuities, like the rediscovery of forgotten women's writing by feminist publishers today. This process has re-introduced various popular novels of the early twentieth century to relatively large numbers of later twentieth century readers, but their readership is based not on bringing Mary Webb or May Sinclair into the literary canon, but on the political interest in women's lives and writings generated by the women's movements in Britain and America. A dualistic model of canonical literature *versus* popular literature, even one which concedes movement between the two categories, is not able to explain the complex negotiations and exchanges which take place over time.

But arguments which dichotomise Literature/the popular as a simple opposition have come under increasing challenge. Not merely because of the evident inadequacy of the popular=bad, escapist side of the antithesis, but also because the notion of 'Literature', as an order of 'timeless monuments' or eternal truths, has itself broken down. In the first half of the twentieth century, it was usual practice to measure popular culture against the threatened but still hegemonic values of the cultural elite. Q.D. Leavis, in her *Fiction and the Reading Public* (1932), argued that a once unified reading public which in the mid-nineteenth century had enjoyed both Dickens *and* George Eliot, had split into an educated and a general public – the one reading Henry James, the other Marie Corelli. She saw this 'impassable gulf' as the effect of the 1870 Education Act, the arrival of cheap editions and a general decline in standards in twentieth century Britain. There is no consideration of the cultural gains produced by increased access to education or reading; her survey of popular reading is geared to mobilise an 'armed and conscious minority' in defence of Literature and traditional culture against the threat not only of best sellers, but also of radio, cinema and advertising. In this story Literature becomes a heroic and embattled David fighting off the Goliath of mass media philistinism.

Twenty-five years later, Richard Hoggart, writing from different political allegiances (and after the 1944 Education Act), was more concerned with the effects of popular culture *on* the majority. Analysing the interplay between material improvement and cultural loss, Hoggart tries to alert his Never-Had-It-So-Good readers to 'the danger of reducing the larger part of the population to a condition of obediently receptive passivity, their eyes glued to television sets, pin-ups, and cinema screens'.[8] What both of these earlier critiques of popular culture have in common is that both employ a static and idealised concept of Literature as the source of supra-historical *value*. Literature is not only opposed to all other media forms, it is set up against and over all other forms of writing.

Left analysis of popular culture in the 1960s and 1970s initially took up the Leavis/Hoggart opposition and tried to re-work it in materialist terms. Literature and the popular were re-defined in terms of their relation to ideology and ideological assumptions about class and gender, but Literature remained the privileged term as in bourgeois criticisms. The underprivileged term (the popular) served, as Virginia Woolf said about women's relation to men, as a looking-glass possessing the magic and delicious power of reflecting the figure of Literature at twice its natural size. For Literature is seen as operating transformatively on ideology, producing a 'knowledge' of it, whereas popular fiction merely reproduces and transmits that ideology. (Thus Balzac's *Comédie Humaine explores* royalist ideology, but Baroness Orczy's *The Scarlet Pimpernel* simply passes it on.) In the realm of Literature, the text's internal operations guarantee to some extent the deconstruction of the ideological, whereas the formulaic structures of popular fiction 'naturalise' the ideological discourses they contain, thus delivering 'uniform, unambiguous and non-contradictory'[9] messages. In other words, formal and aesthetic effects are granted to Art literature but denied to the popular.

These Left critiques, whether Lukácsian, Frankfurt or Althusserian, tend to corroborate the distinctions formed in traditional literary criticism: as Tony Bennett points out, the same body of canonised texts are approved, but for different reasons, and the rest – lumped together as a residue – disapproved; there is the same obsessive concern with the problem of value; and a similar fetishism of the text and textual readings. Non-canonical texts are collapsed back into their conditions of production, and the effects of popular texts are read off from their ideological content. Often, this is particularly the case with discussions of women's popular writing; there is a slide into Left moralism and puritanism about the 'self-indulgence' of 'habitual reading for entertainment'.[10] These left-wing strictures come close at times to the conservative laments of Leavis and earlier critics of the popular. There is little real engagement with the question:

> If, as is frequently argued (for instance in Mills and Boon's own publicity), romance fiction is pure escapism, then why should a housewife, clerical worker or a schoolgirl escape from a world economically and psychologically dominated by men into fictional fantasies of the same thing expressed sexually?[11]

Furthermore, the Literature/popular opposition distorts the way in which writing is historicised. Though the historical relativism of the terms elite/popular is of course argued by Marxists, some critics allow high cultural forms a continuous development, but dogmatically deny this to popular arts: 'The commodity production of contemporary or industrial mass culture has nothing to do, and nothing in common, with older forms of popular and folk art,' writes Fredric Jameson in his essay 'Reification and utopia'.[12]. The emergence of commodity production and a market economy clearly has major implications for the text-reader relationship. But this is as true for literature as 'art' as it is for the popular art forms.[13] The real difference, of form and function, between pre-industrial and post-industrial popular art cannot, it seems to me, be explained by this simple reference to the economic. Nor can they be understood in isolation from the 'high' art forms with which they interact so intimately.

Romance as genre

It is possible to argue about 'romance', as Raymond Williams has about 'tragedy', that the only continuity is in the term: that there is no historical relationship between Greek 'romances', medieval romance, Gothic bourgeois romances of the 1840s, late nineteenth century women's romances and mass-produced romance fiction now – except the generic term. In so far as genres are contracts between a writer and his/her readers, these contracts, and the conventions which go with them, obviously differ according to the conditions of class, ideology and literacy in different social formations. Yet is is also possible, I think, to give some weight to the claim that romance is one of the oldest and most enduring of literary modes which survives today.

As Margaret Williamson argues in her essay on Greek romance, romance evolved in some sense as a *popular* alternative to the major genres of Ancient Greece (though it was also an element in major literary modes like the epic). A non-mimetic prose narrative focusing on emotion, it began when the split between public and private worlds began, when the 'subject' of the Greek *polis* devised new forms in which to speak their 'subjectivity'. Of course, its uses cannot be read off from or confined to this point of origin (suggestive though it is for modern romance forms), and the contribution to this volume by Anna Clark makes a rather different case for 'seduction' romances of nineteenth century England.

Some literary theorists, Northrop Frye for example, have attempted to find an underlying structural unity for different forms of romance, defining it as the literature of wish-fulfilment and claiming that it represents the intrusion of the 'it might have been' into the 'it was'. While the actual world keeps these two, like dreaming and waking, work and play, in continual antithesis, the popular appeal of romance, he says, is that it dissolves the boundaries between the actual and the potential, offering a vision of 'the possible or future or ideal'.[14] While the nature of that 'possible' or 'ideal' will vary with the varying ideological conditions, this utopian vision is, claims Frye, what makes this peripheral and undervalued form so paradoxically central to what writing and reading have to offer. One of the most forceful of the structural theorists of genre, Frye also makes a strong claim for the role of popular forms like romance in literary history. They provide a repertoire of devices from which new formal developments emerge. It was from popular theatre rather than neo-classical drama, he says, that Marlowe and Shakespeare developed, and it was popular ballads and broadsides of the eighteenth century that anticipated the Songs of Innocence and the Lyrical Ballads. 'In prose,' he continues, 'the popular literature signalising such new developments has usually taken the form of a rediscovery of the formulas of romance.'[15]

These theoretical arguments about the continuities or discontinuities of romance or tragedy (indeed of history itself) are necessary but not perhaps sufficient. It is in the detailed historical accounts of the *transformations* of codes and conventions that these questions will be clarified. For if generic forms are, as I argued earlier, signals in a *social* contract between writers and readers, changes in these conventions will be regulated by transformations at other levels of social relationships. Thus for cultural historians, the study of genres may provide a mediation between literary history and social history – one which enables us to break out of the 'splendid isolation' in which traditional histories of literature are confined.

Put another way, to see modern romances as genealogical upstarts, or the bastardised offspring of originally noble forbears, is to reproduce a fantasy of the decline-and-fall type, but does *not* help to explain the evolution of cultural forms. But we can instead ask why the romance has moved from being about a male subject to being about a feminine one;[16] or in what way the tests and trials faced by the hero of medieval romance differ from the obstacles and trials through which the heroine of contemporary romance must typically pass to achieve her object; or how it is that the 'magic' which in earlier romances rescues the hero from false Grails becomes in *Jane Eyre* a supernatural voice which unites her with her 'true' destiny; and why that magic/supernatural/Providential force is in today's romance represented as coming from *within*: as the magic and omnipotent power of sexual desire. A structural and semantic reading of these changing codes necessarily engages with questions of gender, ideology and change.

Thus to approach romance as genre is not to lay claim to some ahistorical quiddity, but may, on the contrary, be to tackle the question of its historical functions. It will, perhaps, be objected here that this has always been the fate of popular fiction: that whereas genre is a backdrop for 'high' cultural productions, genre analysis has dominated the study of popular writing. Among the contributors to this collection, for example, Alison Light has argued that genre study is used to reify popular writing into *en bloc* categories where Barbara Cartland is synonymous with Mills & Boon (or Agatha Christie with Raymond Chandler), regardless of the fact that different and sometimes antithetical readerships are involved. Whilst agreeing that items in popular genres need individualising – her analysis of du Maurier's *Rebecca*, 'Returning to Manderley: female sexuality and class',[17] is a brilliant example of this practice – I'd personally still wish to argue the usefulness of seeing popular texts in relation to genre:

> So generic affiliations, and the systematic deviation
> from them, provide clues which lead us back to the
> concrete historical situation of the individual text
> itself, and allows us to read its structure as ideology,
> as a socially symbolic act, as a prototypical response
> to a historical dilemma.[18]

A somewhat different and more synchronic approach to the genre question is adopted in John Cawelti's *Adventure, Mystery and Romance*, which several contributors here refer to. Cawelti compares the dominant forms of contemporary popular fiction, and identifies the following features of romance: (*a*) the centrality of the love relationship with adventure/incident as subsidiary elements (whereas in the thriller/adventure story, incident is central and love element subsidiary or illustrative); (*b*) in women's romance, the major relationship is between heroine and hero, whereas in male-directed genres it is between hero and villain; (*c*) most contemporary romance has a female protagonist, whereas most adventure stories star a male protagonist; (*d*) romance depends on a special relationship of identification between reader and protagonist whether the narration is in the first or the third person. These points are useful, I think, not only for contemporary romance writing but in thinking through the romance element in the mainstream novel.

When Clara Reeve's *The Progress of Romance* first appeared in 1785, she was concerned to argue the antiquity and universality of romance *against* the newly emerged novel form. For although the Romantics claimed a privileged status for *poetic* discourse, it was a prose form, the novel, which went on to become hegemonic in nineteenth century writing. A prose form claiming to deliver 'truth to life', romance conventions of plot, setting and characterisation were officially excluded as nineteenth century realist aesthetics took shape. But romance elements were not so easily banished, they remained alive and well not only on the margins but in the heartland of the realist novel. Having become established as a 'serious' literary genre (with its own conventions) by the middle of the nineteenth century, the novel as it were also sought to deliver the literary effects – comedy, tragedy and romance – of previously dominant forms. Thus in nineteenth century fiction, romance conventions can be seen not merely in the novels of the Brontës, Dickens and Hardy, but also in Leavis's Great Tradition, Austen, Eliot, James and Conrad. (Jane Austen's novels for example could be said to conform to Cawelti's definitions in almost every respect!) One consequence of this intermingling of modes was that subsequent attempts to use romance show distinct traces of realist influence: simplified plots, complexified characters and naturalised settings. The nineteenth century novel had in effect revealed that far from being always antithetical, romance and realism could become close and compatible literary bedfellows.

Reading popular romance

The mixture of realism and romance in much popular fiction – its reference to both the 'real' and the ideal worlds – gives rise to some complex political effects. Most of the contributors of this collection see an analogy, I think, between their work on popular culture and socialist attempts to understand the popularity of right-wing, conservative politics in

Britain and the US at present. Recent analyses of political populism argue that we have to ask what it is so many identify with in conservative ideology (and *why*); what it is that so many voters and readers seem to give their consent to, or 'give in to'. The traditional socialist answer is of course that mass-media images of power and pleasure seduce people away from reality, from their real interests and needs by substituting false ones. (They vote for Thatcher or Reagan *and* they watch Dynasty and Dallas is one frequently made link.) The Left, in other words, thinks the Right becomes popular by deception, by imposing false consciousness on people's real needs and aspirations. But this manipulation model of explanation leaves us, as socialists, with a very passive and unpromising conception of 'the people'. And as Stuart Hall has argued in another context,[19] conservative ideologies in politics become 'popular' only if they can represent their analysis and programme as the solution to people's interests – real and imaginary, conscious and unconscious. So any socialist alternative which seeks to win consent must dispense with the 'passivity model' in order to understand what *active* needs are being met by the conservative ideologies we wish to displace.

One of the most central and difficult achievements of the women's movement during the 1970s was to re-introduce and re-define notions of subjectivity within Left politics. Under the slogan 'The personal is political', feminists launched their attack on Left 'objectivism' which defined economic issues of wages, conditions and exploitation as *political* but relegated questions of sexuality, subjectivity and the family to the *personal* sphere – outside the scope of political analysis and struggle. If socialist policies were to become desirable to large numbers of so-called 'apolitical' women, it was argued, the Left must learn to articulate demands which would meet the active needs of women in their dual roles in the home and the workplace. Although sections of the male Left were unable to rise to this challenge, feminist arguments about the importance of subjectivity have – theoretically and strategically – had a profound impact on British political thought.

In a parallel way, it was feminists' discontent with the traditional Left view of women romance readers – as masochistic, 'regressive' and passive – which led to new feminist work on romance. Male critics with little or no identification with women readers slide inexorably from denigrations of the text to contempt for the reader. Mistaking the thing on the page for the experience itself, they see popular romance as a packaged commodity relaying false consciousness to an essentially passive and foolish reader. Since 50 per cent of all women reading at any given moment are likely to be reading romance, this is not a construction which can be allowed to stand unchallenged by feminists.

In fact this model of reading is an inadequate and reductive one, Ann Jones claims, in her essay on Mills & Boon romances. Readers of even the most formulaic of mass-produced fantasies for women are much more active and discriminating than this and the political effects of their reading cannot be deduced from the ideology of the text (any more than working class consciousness can be read off from a textual analysis of *The Sun*, one might say). For though the text is a fixed verbal structure, its use or 'meaning' is constituted by socially and historically situated subjects.

Drawing on readership analysis by Janice Radway and others, Jones points out that romance narratives offer the heroine (and reader) the love of a 'strong' male hero, but that this may satisfy a fantasy of being nurtured rather than seduced. The hero's ability to take care of the heroine, while it may reproduce patriarchal role models, may at the same time actually counter most women's real situation, so that 'the heroine is positioned not as victim but as the centre of expert care and attention'. For women whose primary daytime role (in the family or in the workplace) may well be to nurture others, this romance convention can thus represent a utopian aspiration, one which, while it may contain, may equally well *support* any demands made in the real world.

In essays on the family saga as romance and on popular writing in the 1950s, Christine Bridgwood and Alison Light make related points about the plural and contradictory effects of the texts they consider. In her reading of *The Thorn Birds*, *Family Affairs* and *Penmarric*, Christine Bridgwood considers the ways in which one of the newer sub-genres of popular writing has taken on features of both romance and realism. In the saga, unlike romance, marriage is not the closure point to the narrative, but a starting point for new episodes – the story of the next generation. Although, as she says, 'the modern family saga explores the same terrain as the realist novel of the nineteenth century', there are significant differences in the ways the family is represented. The combination of different narrative conventions produces certain incoherencies and tensions which read 'symptomatically'[20] can be seen as symptoms of what the text is unable to repress or reconcile within the story. Thus the saga's attempt to represent the family as the site of purely personal experience – a space beyond social and political conflicts – is frustrated by the 'long view' of the family over several generations. And because the reader is forced to transfer interest and identification from one character or generation to the next, she or he is led beyond individual identification towards a sense of the social, beyond the story of one lifetime towards the question of collective lives in historical process.

The multiple effects – this time of a thriller–detective–

romance – are explored in Alison Light's reading of
The Franchise Affair by Josephine Tey. By locating this
popular detective tale in an analysis of the post-war
reconstruction of the family and the welfare state, she
concentrates on ways in which the different models of
femininity posed within the text are defined and
contrasted via class differences. These conflicting types
of femininity are in turn related to the reorganisation of
British society in this period, she argues, in that 'class
mobility, consumerism and the final collapse of British
Imperial power' are not separable 'from questions of
gender and sexual difference'. Tey's bizarre story,in
which a middle-aged woman and her elderly mother
are accused of imprisoning a young schoolgirl and
beating her into becoming their maid, is analysed in
some detail in order to suggest that not only is the text
thematically and formally contradictory, but that it
addresses the equally divided and contradictory subjectivity of the reader.

One of the most interesting points, I think, to
emerge from recent feminist readings of popular
romance has been this emphasis that texts do not speak
to a unified feminine reading subject, but to a divided,
contradictory and bisexual one. Drawing on psychoanalytic and semiological theories of subjectivity and
representation, these readings stress the ways in which
fundamental divisions of psychic life and the importance
of fantasy affect the politics of reading. The repressions
and repetitions in the textual system cannot therefore
be construed merely as 'artistic flaws' but are evidence
of these always-existing conflicts in both our inner and
outer worlds. The contradictory representation of
homosexuality, for example, which I discuss in my
essay on *The Well of Loneliness*, is relevant to the failure
and difficulty that *many* women experience in unifying
their polymorphous sexual drives into the recognised
patterns of 'femininity' in our society.

The splitting of characters into heroines and villains, good and bad objects, which is so typical of romance, is frequently ridiculed. It has also been criticised because it relieves the reader of the struggle with complexity, the struggle to unite the good and the bad into a whole object which is the project of realist fictions. In her discussion of contemporary feminist writing, Michele Roberts argues that the splitting of bad and good qualities into, respectively, male and female characters has become a constricting convention which the feminist writer must now move beyond. Gender stereotyping of this sort, she suggests, inhibits the exploration of femininity and its complexities and is liberating for neither writer nor reader.

The polarisations offered in melodrama, fantasy and romance fictions may certainly refer us back to (psychologically) primitive ways of seeing the world, but whether this 'regressive' experience is a positive or a negative one is again determined not by the romance itself but by the interaction of text and context. Recent studies of romance discuss this issue in some depth. Janice Radway,[21] despite caveats, argues that reading romances has an integrative and enabling effect on women's lives. Tania Modleski,[22] on the other hand, is more dubious about romance's ability to relieve ambivalence and anxiety. The American Harlequin series she says, may actually 'induce' or 'intensify' women's conflicts just as 'certain tranquillisers taken to relieve anxiety are, though temporarily helpful, ultimately anxiety producing. The user must constantly increase the dosage of the drug in order to alleviate problems aggravated by the drug itself.'

Different kinds of divisions are addressed in Helen Taylor's reading of *Gone With the Wind*. The resourcefulness and energy of Scarlett O'Hara may provide a liberating experience for white women readers, while reinforcing reactionary racial stereotypes for black women. In a forceful argument against uncritical celebrations of this 'classic' 1930s romance, she comments that 'for a reader to celebrate the text's feminism must involve both turning a blind eye to its white supremacist southern propaganda, and entering into an unholy alliance with the crudest southern chauvinism and the activities of the Ku Klux Klan.' The divisive effects of white racism upon the American women's movement, she points out, should make us doubly careful about ways of reading such romances.

The ways in which romance has been used to represent national and community aspirations is the subject of Derrick Price's essay on Llewellyn's *How Green Was My Valley*. The history of the Welsh valleys is used as a myth, he suggests, to construct a 'romance of Wales' in which class antagonisms are displaced in favour of an appeal to a unified national identity – a particularly relevant theme in 1939. The romance element serves to harness community feeling to a nostalgic and patriarchal fantasy of Welshness. His argument contrasts with that of Anna Clark on early nineteenth century tales of seduction where popular fiction and popular politics share a radical critique of class and power relations, and where, she claims, the romance theme supports this radicalism.

The final essay in this collection is by a writer of fiction. At the History Workshop conference for which most of these essays were originally prepared, writers as well as readers exchanged views and argued the politics of popular fiction. One of the pleasures of that meeting was in breaking down male-female, popular-elite, writer-reader barriers. So because we felt this collection would not be complete (or would be more incomplete) without the voice of a contemporary writer, we asked the feminist novelist Michele Roberts to give her view of romance and the writer.

A final ('the clinch') point: it is often stated that in

the twentieth century, literature, both art and popular, has taken on the functions of religion in the nineteenth. Marx said about religion not only that it was the opium of people, but also – in a phrase most people remember only from John Cornford's poem – that it was 'the heart of the heartless world'.[23] I think this is true – not of the popular texts themselves, but of what their readers bring to them. For the desire to change life for the better may not be concentrated into a single conscious political channel, but may be dispersed into many rivulets and deltas, the network of available forms. In so far as popular romance represents many of our deepest fantasies, about social as well as individual satisfaction, it deserves our attention so that we can, as Alison Light says in her essay, 'achieve a more compassionate and generous understanding of human consciousness and its effects, and of how political changes come about.'

Notes

1 Cawelti, John G., *Adventure, Mystery and Romance*, University of Chicago Press, Chicago, 1976.
2 Hall, Stuart, 'Notes on deconstructing the popular', *People's History and Socialist Theory*, ed. Raphael Samuel, London, Routledge & Kegan Paul, 1981, p.228.
3 Sebestyen, Amanda, 'A taste for S & F', *City Limits*, no.191, May 1985; Hill, Dave, 'Opinions', *City Limits*, no.197, July 1985.
4 Bennett, Tony, 'Marxism and popular fiction', *Literature and History*, vol.VII, no.2, Autumn 1981.
5 Williams, Raymond, *Keywords*, Oxford, Oxford University Press, 1976, p.230.
6 Frye, Northrop, *The Secular Scripture*, Cambridge, Mass., Harvard University Press, 1976, p.28.
7 The Russian formalist Shklovsky also held that new art forms were 'simply the canonisation of inferior (sub-literary) genres',

cited in Wellek, R. and Warren, A., *Theory of Literature*, London, Penguin, 1949, p.235.

8 Hoggart, Richard, *The Uses of Literacy*, Harmondsworth, Penguin, 1957, p.316.

9 Bromley, Roger, 'Natural boundaries:the social function of popular fiction', *Red Letters*, no.7, 1977.

10 Margolies, David, 'Mills and Boon, Guilt without Sex', *Red Letters*, no.14, 1982.

11 McNeil, Helen, 'She trembled at his touch', *Quarto*, no.17.

12 Jameson, Fredric, 'Reification and utopia in mass culture', *Social Text*, vol.1, no.1, 1979 p.134.

13 Christopher Pawling makes a very similar point in *Popular Fiction and Social Change*, London, Macmillan, 1984.

14 Frye, Northrop, *The Secular Scripture*, p.58 and p.179ff.

15 Ibid., p.28

16 See Mitchell, Juliet, *The Longest Revolution*, London, Virago, 1984, p.108.

17 Light, Alison, 'Returning to Manderley: female sexuality and class', *Feminist Review*, no.16, 1984.

18 Jameson, Fredric, 'Magical narratives: romance as genre', *New Literary History*, vol.VII, 1975, p.157.

19 A discussion between Stuart Hall and Tony Benn at 'Left Alive', a *Marxism Today* conference, held on 3–4 November 1984 at the City University, London.

20 The term is used by Pierre Macherey in *A Theory of Literary Production*, London, Routledge & Kegan Paul, 1978.

21 Radway, Janice, 'Women read the romance', *Feminist Studies*, vol.9, no.1, Spring 1985.

22 Modleski, Tania, *Loving with a Vengeance*, New York, Methuen, 1984, p.57.

23   'Religious distress is at the same time the *expression* of real distress and also a *protest* against real distress. Religion is the sigh of the oppressed creature, the heart of the heartless world, just as it is the spirit of spiritless conditions. It is the *opium* of the people.' ('Contribution to the critique of Hegel's philosophy of law', Marx-Engels, *Collected Works*, vol.3, London, Lawrence & Wishart, 1975, p.175.)

Cornford, John, 'Poem', *Spanish Civil War Verse*, Harmonds-worth, Penguin, 1980, p.110.

Frontispiece engraving from George Thornley's translation of
Daphnis and Chloe, published in 1657 (British Library)

2
The Greek romance

MARGARET WILLIAMSON

The romance, the last new genre produced by classical antiquity, has had a bad press. Macaulay's dismissal was absolute: on his copy of one of the five surviving Greek romances he wrote 'Detestable trash', and on another 'A most stupid, worthless performance'. A modern critic, after the more moderate observation that 'the demerits of the Greek romances are clear', sums it up as follows: 'Cardboard lovers, buffeted by Fate, drift on a stream of sentimental rhetoric . . . through predictable perils, to a predictable happy ending. The categories are those of the B-feature Western: the fag end of epic.'[1] The full-scale, straight-faced versions of romance are all Greek: in Latin literature it has left its trace only in the parodies by Petronius and Apuleius,[2] and in occasional disdainful references by Roman litterati. Literary theorists such as Horace and Quintilian do not so much as mention it; and there is no generic name for it in either Latin or Greek, despite its instantly recognisable, stereotyped plot.

One reason for its low status in antiquity is the fact that it offends against the decorum of genre. The Greek romances are all written in prose, which was traditionally the medium for serious, particularly historical, writing. Lucian, in *How to Write History*, is voicing the orthodox view when he castigates those who fail to distinguish between history, whose province is to tell the truth and whose purpose is utility, and fiction, which aims merely to please and should be confined strictly to poetry. The emperor Julian, in recommending the reading of history to priests, also went out of his way to exclude fiction masquerading as history – that is, 'love stories and . . . all such stuff'. Modern readers bring to the romance a different set of expectations which are equally liable to be disappointed. For a reader reared on the nineteenth century novel it is difficult to tolerate the romance writers' complete lack of interest in character or in the plausibility of events, and the absence of any social or moral context for their protagonists' actions. Northrop Frye, in *The Secular Scripture*, describes the difficulty of approaching a romantic novelist such as Walter Scott from a standpoint based on the very different realistic tradition of the novel, and much of what he says applies closely to the Greek romances.[3]

In the case of the Greek romances there are, I think, additional difficulties which arise from the use of a form which is a relic from the past for material completely unsuited to it. I shall return to this point later; but it is important to note that critical disparagement of these works was not shared by the reading public. The number and distribution of papyrus finds suggest, on the contrary, that they had considerable popularity among a population sufficiently literate (unlike those of earlier times) to read them fairly easily. They were also widely imitated later, not only by Byzantine Greeks in the twelfth century, but also in the Renaissance, when Heliodorus, the latest of the romance writers, was printed in Greek and then translated into French, German, Spanish, Italian and English within the space of forty years. At this point the romance seems at last to have become respectable.[4]

The genre is interesting, however, precisely because

in its own time it seems to have developed separately from, or on the fringes of, the mainstream of 'high' literature. Like many of its protagonists, whose noble birth is often concealed until the final denouement, the romance has been the subject of much enquiry as to its origins: it has been explained variously as the product of religious cult, school exercises in rhetoric and 'love-interest' episodes in historical writing. But unlike the well-born lovers in whom it specialises, the romance has no such pure and easily unmasked origins: the most convincing explanation of its genesis is that it is merely one version of widespread, traditional story material in a culture much given to storytelling. It is true that pairs of lovers make regular appearances in earlier historical writing – the historian Xenophon's Panthea and Abradatas are the best-known example – and that the author of our earliest complete romance, Chariton, is precise and accurate about the historical setting of his story. But other motifs which are the romance's stock-in-trade – wanderings in foreign parts, capture by pirates, nobly born distressed maidens sold into slavery and then rescued – are found in other, widely differing sources, oriental as well as Greek. The learned disquisitions, descriptions and allusions with which the authors of the five extant romances often lard their naratives cannot conceal the stereotyped, and already ancient, nature of their basic material.[5]

The romances of which we have complete texts were all written by and for the Greek-speaking population of the eastern Roman Empire, in the first, second and third centuries AD, a time of relative political stability, though also of nostalgia for Greece's gloriously independent past. Of their authors we know very little: unlike the Roman parodists Petronius and Apuleius, they do not seem to have been prominent figures. The romance formula can be seen in its simplest form in the two earliest writers, Chariton and Xenophon of

Ephesus, and it is on their versions that I shall concentrate to begin with. The three later writers, while still clearly dependent on the formula, all vary it in some way. Achilles Tatius' version, with its absurdly frequent digressions and often gruesome sensationalism, suggests a certain distancing of the author from the demands of the plot; Longus produces a cross between romance and pastoral; and Heliodorus draws out his labyrinthine plot with sustained virtuosity.[6]

The plot of Chariton's romance is, in outline, as follows. His protagonists, Chaereas and Callirhoe, fall in love on the first page and marry, by popular demand, on the second. But an estrangement is soon engineered by Callirhoe's other suitors. In a moment of rage Chaereas kicks Callirhoe, who appears to die and is entombed. Pirates then rob the tomb, take the now revived Callirhoe to Miletus, and sell her to the steward of its governor, Dionysius. (Miletus is at this time part of the Persian Empire, which is the setting for most of the rest of the story until the lovers finally return to independent Syracuse; this gives occasion for frequent anti-barbarian sentiments on the author's part.) Dionysius is smitten by Callirhoe, who despite her loyalty to Chaereas agrees to marry him for the sake of Chaereas' child, with which she now finds herself pregnant.

Chaereas meanwhile discovers the truth about the tomb robbery, sets out for Miletus in search of Callirhoe and soon falls upon hard times. He has barely had time to come across a statue of Callirhoe, the discovery of which shows him that he is on the right track, when he is attacked by barbarians, sold as a slave to Mithridates, governor of Caria, implicated in a slave revolt and sentenced to death by crucifixion. He does not particularly mind this, since like all the lovers he would rather die than live without his beloved.

However, as luck and narrative convention would have it, Mithridates has seen and fallen in love with Callirhoe, so when he discovers Chaereas' identity he rescues him in the hope of eventually using him to further his suit with Callirhoe. As a result of a complicated series of coincidences Dionysius discovers that Mithridates has designs on Callirhoe and appeals for help to his superior Pharnaces, governor of Lydia; but this is not much good because Pharnaces too is in love with Callirhoe. They all depart for the Persian capital to seek arbitration by the Persian king Artaxerxes.

The reader is by now only slightly surprised to find that Artaxerxes has outdone them all in having fallen in love with Callirhoe by hearsay. This complicates the trial which follows, since Artaxerxes is reluctant to award her to anyone at all, even Dionysius and Chaereas who both think they are married to her. The resulting stalemate is ended by the outbreak of war, in which Chaereas fights for the Egyptians against Artaxerxes and eventually captures an island to which Callirhoe happens to have been sent for safety. They are reunited; Callirhoe makes it all up to Dionysius by leaving him the child which he believes to be his; and she and Chaereas return to Syracuse to a rapturous public welcome.

The structure of Xenophon's *Ephesian Tale* is very similar. He too has his lovers, Habrocomes and Anthia, vanquished by Love and married within the first few pages; but as an oracle has already outlined the plot for them they begin lamenting right away, load a boat with pirate-tempting treasures and set sail. Separations and adventures of every description then follow until, on the last page, we find them, as expected, in bed together delicately checking up on each other's fidelity. The only significant difference between their adventures and those of Chariton's lovers is a greater degree of symmetry between their experiences: Habrocomes as well as Anthia is the object of unwelcome attentions – including a homosexual approach from a pirate captain – and Anthia finds herself in danger of her life almost as often as Habrocomes. As in Chariton, the convoluted coincidences upon which the plot depends are attributed to the god of Love or to the deity Chance, and as in Chariton the lovers spend many a page lamenting their fate and longing, implausibly, for death.

One does not need to refer to the résumé which Apollo's oracle so obligingly provides in Xenophon's version in order to see from these two examples both how stereotyped the plot is and how completely it takes precedence over any considerations of verisimilitude or of consistency in characterisation. Chariton's character Mithridates, for example, appears to forget his love for Callirhoe and depart from the scene as soon as it is convenient to the author that he should do so: his only role was to swell the ranks of her admirers and provide more twists in the plot. Hippothoos in Xenophon's version can for similar reasons make his first appearance as a brigand capable of incarcerating the heroine in a pit with wild dogs, and finish up as the lovers' friend and ally, without any comment by the author on his moral metamorphosis; nor does Xenophon seem to think it at all inappropriate that the hero, Habrocomes, should join Hippothoos' robber band at the end of book 2, even though robber bands are one of a lover's regular perils. The predictability of the formula is interestingly revealed in Xenophon by some of his slips in construction. I have already mentioned his lovers' collusion with their author in the matter of the oracle: far from trying to avert the forecast danger, they seem to be doing their utmost to invite it by making their boat as tempting a prey as possible. Later on they each, in the belief that the other is dead, utter the usual demands for instant death; but so far is the author from expecting us to take this seriously that he sometimes forgets to disabuse them of their mistake before setting them off on their quest again.

The demands of the plot give rise to other difficulties too in taking the lovers' emotions seriously. The *raison d'être* of the entire narrative is, of course, their love for each other; but as long as the story lasts it can be satisfied only briefly, if at all. The reason for this is articulated by several characters within the text, and most interestingly in Chariton by a eunuch belonging to the Persian king. Observing his master's lovesickness, he makes the obvious comment that it is only Callirhoe's inaccessibility that renders her more desirable than the king's own wife: for, he says, 'the fact of possession puts an end to passion'. Since the king cannot be reasoned out of his infatuation, the eunuch suggests possession of Callirhoe as a cure for his desire. The king, in reply, refuses to disobey the laws over which he presides, but in so doing he is, of course, obeying the laws of the narrative scrupulously: not only is he not Callirhoe's legitimate lover, but her possession by anyone at this point would put an end to the story as well as to the passion. It is desire, not its realisation, which is the subject of the narrative, and this requires that the lovers be separated – whether by scruple, physical absence, or divine edict – throughout the story.

If the lovers cannot enjoy each other for as long as the tale lasts, neither can they have any other experience. The enjoyment of love may itself be, for the moment, unavailable; but in that it is defined as the only thing of any importance, it robs all other events in the lovers' lives of significance. The extremes of misery to which all the romance writers subject their protagonists can be seen as an attempt to break through the incapacity for experience which is the consequence of their implacable fidelity. Achilles Tatius notoriously carries these extremes farther than anyone else, and it is hard not to see his treatment as a humorous comment on the demands of the genre: he has his heroine killed twice before her lover – once by disembowelling, once by beheading – and does not enlighten either him or the reader about the way in which the illusion was produced until later.

The lovers' constant emotional excesses also read to some extent like a ludicrous attempt on the part of their authors to allow the characters some of the richness of experience which the plot denies them. The behaviour of Chariton's Chaereas is a fair sample: he resolves to set sail in search of his lost bride's body, but then spends the voyage weeping with his head covered, so that he does not even notice when his boat approaches that of the pirates who have sold her into captivity. Later, after discovering that she is in fact alive, he is about to set off again when his aged parents plead with him not to leave them. His mother, making her one and only appearance in the book, asks to be taken on board on condition that they may throw her overboard as soon as she becomes *de trop*. Her son's reaction to this is instant and extreme: he himself leaps overboard on the spot and has to be fished out by his crew before the voyage can commence.

The lovers' supreme virtue, their fidelity, has parallel consequences as regards the possibility of moral choice. Their unswerving loyalty to each other, proof against any torture, is devalued by the fact that it is arbitrary: the hero's passion for the heroine is distinguished from that of (usually) innumerable other men only by its arbitrary legitimacy. Since this legitimacy is conferred by the author, albeit in the name of Eros, and not chosen by the protagonists, no real virtue can attach to it. And yet the absolute value placed upon fidelity renders any other virtue impossible: the lovers can and do lie, cheat and manipulate their way out of any situation with only the occasional passing glance at such things as filial piety (once *en route*, Chaereas forgets his mother for good) or religious observance. Angela Carter's observation about de Sade's sexually pure victim figure Justine is equally true of these lovers: they too are all 'incapable of judgement and, in that sense, beyond good and evil'; their stories too illustrate 'the moral limitations of a life conducted solely according to the virtuous promptings of the heart'.[7]

The moral and emotional insensibility which they share with Justine extends in their case even to love itself. This is, as I have said, the only relationship of any significance; yet for these lovers it is both a completely passive and a completely egocentric experience. Love is presented as an automatic and irresistible reaction to beauty, which accounts for the way in which the faultless looks of hero and heroine strew the pages with conquests. The meeting of Habrocomes and Anthia is typical: Anthia 'caught the beauty of Habrocomes, which flowed into her eyes', and Habrocomes, who has declared himself immune to love, it is at once 'the god's bound prisoner'. Achilles Tatius, who is particularly fond of physico-psychological digressions, devotes several to love, which is always an optical rather than a spiritual event:

> The pleasure which comes from vision enters by the eyes and makes its home in the breast; bearing with it ever the image of the beloved, it impresses it upon the mirror of the soul and leaves there its image; the emanation given off by beauty travels by invisible rays to the lovesick heart and imprints upon it its form. (263)

It is entirely in keeping with this view of things that

Chariton's Dionysius should do his utmost to prevent Callirhoe from weeping for Chaereas – not out of sympathy for her, but 'fearing that her beauty might . . . suffer thereby'. Justine fears above all things not rape but seduction and the loss of self entailed thereby. The view of love articulated by Achilles Tatius and shared by all the romance writers makes such a loss of self impossible for their characters: love itself is more like rape than anything else – a violent event which assails them from outside and utterly overpowers them. Since, however, their inter-action with anyone but the beloved is minimal, this means that they are isolated within a solipsistic world.

It might be objected at this point that what I have been doing is applying to these stories criteria derived from the tradition of realistic narrative; and there is no reason why they should pass such a test. Certainly the same problems do not arise in the case of the romantic cameos such as that of Panthea and Abradatas, which I mentioned earlier. But the authors of these full-blown romances invite such criticism largely because of the form in which they have chosen to develop their material. The formal antecedents of the romances are epic and drama, with rhetoric as a later addition. As in epic, the tale is told using a high proportion of direct speech, messages are quoted (or misquoted) verbatim, and internal conflict is expressed in the form of debate. Chariton for one shows his awareness of, and pride in, this inheritance by sprinkling his narrative with quotations from Homer. The presence of drama – New Comedy as well as tragedy – as a model for construction is also evident, but only the latter, nobler mode is claimed by the writers, especially by Achilles Tatius and Heliodorus, who even has one of his characters accuse another of having 'come across the sea to stage another Attic tragedy against me'. The third component, rhetoric, is visible not only in the elaborate style of the lovers' constant laments and deliberations but also in the frequency of scenes set in law courts and public assemblies of various kinds.

The Greek romance in its developed form embodies, therefore, some paradoxes. On one hand it is based on folktale material, written by obscure authors and scorned by the literary establishment, but it has a wide readership. Its status as popular literature is also confirmed by the form in which it was reproduced: manuscripts tend to be in codex (early book) form, rather than on the papyrus rolls which were still used for high literature. On the other, the narrative tradition to which it still clearly belongs in formal terms is that of the major genres of classical Greece – epic and drama.

In any attempt to situate the romance within this tradition, the ancestor which the romance writers themselves neglect to claim – New Comedy – turns out to be just as important as the more prestigious tragedy. If we place epic, tragedy and New Comedy in chronological sequence, one of the patterns which emerges is that of the gradual differentiation of the private sphere from the public, and then its usurpation of the central role. It is arguable that a conception of private as distinct from public life barely exists in Homer: the household of a ruler and his wife – Odysseus and Penelope, for example – is at the centre of the political structure, and the importance of this central relationship to the entire community is one of the subjects of the *Odyssey*. In the fifth century, however, the organisation of the Athenian *polis* created a sharp distinction between public, political life and domestic life, which was now completely privatised and to which, of course, women were confined. The single most convincing explanation for the prominence of women in tragedy is that it is a response to this split and to the strains and tensions associated with it.[8] By the time we come to Euripides, the latest of the three major tragedians, however, interest in private, individual experience for its own sake has begun to displace wider social and political issues: the complaint humorously made against him in Aristophanes' play *The Frogs* – that he portrays lovelorn women, cripples and beggars instead of the old upstanding military heroes – is in fact an acute response to this change. The contraction of interest continues into New Comedy, which concentrates exclusively on the relationships between a small group of private individuals, and in which any sense of a wider context is lacking. Because they are so self-contained, the plots of New Comedy have travelled much better than those of tragedy, and elements from them such as aristocratic foundlings, pairs of ill-starred lovers and shipwrecks have persisted not only into these romances but also into European literature.

However, despite the overall shift from public to private which can be traced through these genres, there is one respect in which they are all still biased towards the public expression of shared experience: that is, they are all designed for oral performance at large public gatherings. One reason why Greek epic contains so much direct speech is that it was composed not for solitary reading but for dramatic performance by a bard or rhapsode; and we have a vivid account of the effect such a performance could have on a mass audience in Plato's dialogue the *Ion*. It is no accident that such a situation did not produce much exploration of unique, private and solitary experience, but that on the contrary the focus in tragedy and epic is on experiences which are commonly shared and which can be easily expressed in the public, quasi-official discourse of poetry.[9] In their heyday these genres concentrated on the individual only in the context of an exploration of the nexus of social, moral, political and religious realities of which she or he was a part. The unsatisfactory thinness of the Greek romances arises partly from the fact that their intense contraction of focus on to individual experience – to the extent that even the lovers' relations normally play a very small part in their lives – is not matched by any development of a sense of interiority or by the resources for exploring it: they are still using structures and techniques derived from a tradition which is in fact quite alien to their interests.

The overlaying of these older traditions with the art of rhetoric, which is equally geared to public expression, does not help matters. Even when immured in caves, thrown into pits or confined in prison, the lovers are always playing to an audience, and they do not seem to notice the empty seats. Here is Callirhoe, pregnant by Chaereas, wondering how to respond to Dionysius' offer of marriage:

> Going up to her chamber and shutting the door,
> Callirhoe held the image of Chaereas beneath her
> heart and said, 'Behold, we are three – husband,
> wife and child! Let us plan together what is best for
> us all. I shall first reveal my purpose. . . . But you,
> my child, what do you choose for yourself? . . . It is
> a contrary vote you cast against me, my child. . . .
> But let us enquire also of your father. . . . (32–3)

Achilles Tatius' hero Clitophon, lacking even unborn relatives to whom to address himself, virtually has to dismember himself in order to get an audience: on first entering Alexandria and seeing its wonders, he exclaims, 'Eyes, we are beaten.'

It is true that Homeric heroes also address a reified part of themselves – their *thumos*, roughly translatable as 'heart' or 'spirit' – as a way of representing inner conflict. But even Homer has other resources too for conveying more complex mental states: inner turmoil can be suggested by similes, and conflicting impulses by the intervention of a god, as when Athene restrains Achilles in book 1 of the *Iliad* by pulling his hair. And his interest is rarely confined to the mental state of his heroes: their experiences always relate to a larger arena. The gods are not just ways of representing inner conflict; they also have an independent existence as part of the irreducibly other universe in which a human being finds himself.

The richness of these techniques even in Homer shows up by contrast the poverty of the romance writers' resources. Their images are sparse and clichéd, and the gods have degenerated into mere manipulators of the plot. Condemned to prolonged separation from the only audience which counts, these lovers continue none the less to address thin air, and it is not surprising that they rise to bombastic heights in the vain attempt to make an impression on it. In the sense that this narrative tradition seems in their endless speechifying to have reached a point of exhaustion, the romances fit Northrop Frye's definition of them as 'primitive' literature.

From a literary–historical point of view, then, the Greek romance was a genre whose time was either long past or had not yet come, depending on how you look at it. The avid readers of the first few centuries AD do not seem, however, to have realised this. It is tantalising that we have no information about exactly who they were, let alone any record of their reactions; the only clues to what engaged their interest are those provided by the texts themselves.

One thing which does seem clear, and which distinguishes these romances from their modern descendants, is that the readership was not exclusively female. Xenophon's first translator, Mr. Rooke, addresses his preface without hesitation to his 'fair

Readers'; but neither Xenophon himself nor any of the other authors singles out an audience in this way. The only possible exception to this is an aside from Chariton, who adds to his account of an assembly in Syracuse the information that women could participate in it. Since this detail is both incidental to the plot and (almost certainly) historically inaccurate, it seems to be a ploy by Xenophon to involve his female audience more fully in the sad spectacle of Chaereas' trial which then follows. But it does not indicate that they were the only audience, and in the romances as a whole there is scope for readers of either sex to identify with the protagonists: roughly the same space is allotted to the tribulations of hero and heroine, and in endurance, resourcefulness and verbosity they are more or less equal. Some sexual double standards exist: homosexual attraction occurs only between men; women who make advances to the hero usually turn into vengeful monsters when rebuffed; and lapses in physical – though never, of course, spiritual – fidelity are normally confined to men. But these asymmetries are far fewer than the realities of contemporary life would lead us to expect: given the actual legal and economic status of women,[10] the equality and independence of the lovers is one of the clearest indications that the romances are the product of fantasy.

The political relations of the time too are either absent or transmuted beyond recognition. Only the domination of the lovers' lives by powerful external forces matches in any way the experience of their readers, even though the actual agents of that domination, the Romans, are replaced by Eros or by Chance. Chariton's contempt for barbarians is based on a long-standing Greek prejudice; but the assumption of racial superiority passes into the realm of fantasy with the conquest by Callirhoe – not only a Greek, but a woman – of the Persian king, a man whose power in classical times was so legendary that it was enough to refer to him simply as 'The King'. The treatment of crowds – 'the people' – also embodies a good deal of wish-fulfilment. Their enthusiastic identification with the lovers' interests – they are always obligingly at hand to prostrate themselves before their beauty, demand their marriage, plead for their lives and eventually welcome them back home – suggests a vision of unproblematic aristocratic leadership which was far removed from reality.

In a narrative so governed by fantasy, the absence of a moral dimension to the lovers' actions is perhaps not such a disadvantage. The reader can experience vicariously a potentially endless (since there is no inbuilt structural limit to them) sequence of thrills, secure in the knowledge that no choice, and therefore no guilt, attaches to them, and that a thoroughly respectable outcome – wedded bliss – is guaranteed. The importance of conformity to this norm is shown in Xenophon by the inclusion of an episode which bears no structural relation to the plot but which seems to be there as a kind of ghoulish celebration of married fidelity. One of Habrocomes' last exploits before being reunited with Anthia is a meeting with Aegialeus, an old fisherman who in his youth swore undying love to the girl with whom he eloped. His loyalty has extended even beyond the grave: he has embalmed her corpse and now enjoys a sub-necrophiliac relationship with it, kissing it, talking to it and taking meals in its company. Habrocomes draws out the moral for us: 'true love has no limits of age'.

But the other problems inherent in the romance's structure are more intractable. Nothing can disguise the difficulty presented to an author by the requirement that plot and lovers alike should progress inexorably from A to A. To the problem of making the intervening period both eventful and without effect

Chariton and Xenophon have no solution. In the three later writers the sexual union of the lovers is delayed until the end, which gives the reader something at least slightly different to look forward to; but otherwise their success in giving the story any kind of forward impetus is varied. Achilles Tatius' treatment of the problem is parodic: his lovers manage to get into bed together as early as book 2, and are only prevented from bringing about a premature climax to the tale by the unexpected arrival of Leucippe's mother. Heliodorus' solution is more radical and more successful. He attacks the structural problem by the simple expedient of not beginning at A: the reader is plunged straight into the middle of the lovers' journey without explanation, and is only in a position to reconstruct what has gone before more than halfway through, after a complex series of tales within tales, flashbacks and narrative red herrings

But it is Longus who achieves the most complete and satisfying solution, and he does it by modifying the romance formula to such an extent that we may in the end doubt whether his story belongs to the same genre. The story of Daphnis and Chloe takes place against the background of a pastoral landscape steeped in Greek religious and literary tradition.[11] They are foundlings who are discovered being suckled by a she-goat and a ewe respectively, brought up by rustics and set to herd animals – he, naturally, goats, and she sheep. This they do in the manner of Theocritean shepherds, with much playing of pipes and of pastoral games. Most of the narrative concerns the growth of their love for each other, which is only infrequently interrupted by such familiar events as marauding armies and shipwrecks. Eventually their aristocratic origins are, of course, discovered and they marry; but being the stuff of fable rather than of everyday life, they return to the countryside for the wedding and live out their idyll there.

In the prelapsarian world of their adopted surroundings, Daphnis and Chloe can be permitted to spend most of their days in each other's company because they are separated by an agent far more powerful than any pirate – namely their sexual innocence. It is their wondering incomprehension at the awakening of desire, presented with collusive *faux-naïveté* on the author's part, which ensures the postponement of their union until the end, and thus allows the ostensible subject of all the romances – love – to occupy the foreground. A phrase used of love early in the book suggests, indeed, that the usual ravages of pirates and robbers function in the other romances as a substitute for the erotic experience which has had to be deferred until the 'happy ever after'. Daphnis, his desire newly awakened by the sight of Chloe's nakedness, is so uncomprehending of this sensation that he fancies himself still in the hands of the pirates from whom he has just escaped: for, says Longus, he was 'young and a rustic, and as yet ignorant of the piratical ways of love'.

Since, left to themselves, Daphnis and Chloe experience desire only as incomprehensible pain, their gradual initiation into love's mysteries requires the intervention of several external agencies. The first of these is Eros himself, appearing in richly symbolic guise. In an encounter with the old cowherd Philetas, who relates it to the lovers, Eros both appears as the mischievous boy familiar from Hellenistic literature and claims the cosmic power attributed to him by an older, pre-classical tradition. Philetas elaborates:

A god is Eros, my children . . . he possesses greater power than Zeus himself. He rules the elements, he rules the stars, he rules his fellow deities. . . . All flowers are the work of Eros; all these plants are his handiwork; it is through him that rivers flow and breezes blow.(22)

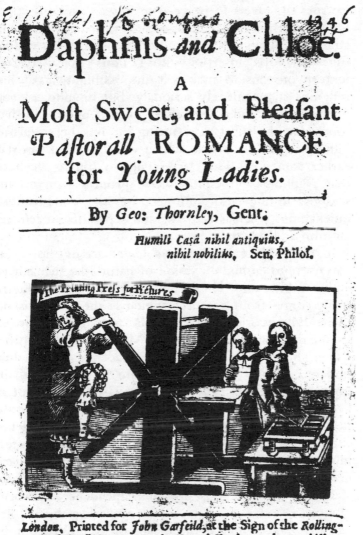

Daphnis and Chloe.

A

Most Sweet, and Pleasant Pastorall ROMANCE for Young Ladies.

By Geo: Thornley, Gent.

Humili Casâ nihil antiquius,
nihil nobilius. Sen, Philof.

The Printing Press for Pictures

London, Printed for John Garfeild, at the Sign of the Rolling-Preſſe for Pictures near the Royal-Exchange in Cornhill, over againſt Popes-Head-Alley, 1657.

Title page of George Thornley's translation of *Daphnis and Chloe*, published in 1657 (British Library)

The immediate purpose of this formidable deity is to instruct the lovers to proceed to 'kisses, embraces and lying together with naked bodies' as a cure for their strange feelings; but he also has another, wider, function. Eros' insertion into Longus' many-layered texture of allusion makes it impossible to take his religious status entirely seriously; but his power over natural world and lovers alike, even if only a literary topos, has the effect of restoring the link between the individual and the world which was missing from the earlier romances. The clearest sign of this is the fact that Daphnis' and Chloe's love progresses with the seasons: spring and summer are the time of its quickening, whereas setbacks and separations occur in autumn and winter.

In this respect *Daphnis and Chloe* seems, however playfully, to embody a vision of natural love; but it is an incomplete one. The second agent of their enlightenment comes from a source which is the antithesis of their idyllic world, and which has been foreshadowed by the description of the city of Mytilene prefacing the story. In book 3 the lovers have got as far as understanding that they must imitate the mating of their goats and sheep, but they are baffled by the differences between human and quadruped anatomy. Daphnis is now seduced by a city woman, Lycaenion, who simultaneously satisfies her own desire and educates him; so that pastoral innocence is ultimately seen to need the sophistication of the city.

This episode reveals an interdependence between innocence and experience which underlies the whole narrative, and which is the means of Longus' triumph in adapting the structure of romance. The lovers' ignorance of love, dispelled progressively by Eros and Lycaenion, is also set in constant ironic counterpoint to the reader's knowledge. It is the gap between the two which allows the engagement of the reader's fantasy and desire, and thereby provides the tale's forward movement: we can recognise and savour Daphnis and Chloe's fledgling passion at the same time as desiring and anticipating its fulfilment. Longus has thus succeeded, as no other of the romance writers has, in making desire both the subject and the dynamic of his narrative.

The pleasure of this recognition is paralleled by another to which the consciousness of sophistication is no less important: that of the learned reader in the centuries of poetic tradition which play upon the text. Longus' allusions are an integral part of his version of romance, and it is his teasing and ironic use of them which saves the lovers' naivety from absurdity. In this sense his romance-pastoral has rejoined learned and literary tradition; here too innocence is dependent on experience, and the end of Greek literature upon its beginning.

Notes

1 P. Parsons, 'Ancient Greek romances', *New York Review of Books*, 20 August–2 September 1981.

2 In Petronius' satire *The Satyricon* a homosexual, and far from idealised, pair of lovers take the place of the heterosexual couple of romance proper, but go through many of the same motions – separation, shipwreck, lamentation – all of which are mercilessly parodied. There is also some parody of romance in Apuleius' comic novel *The Golden Ass*, adapted from a Greek original. The best introduction to both works is P.G. Walsh, *The Roman Novel*, Cambridge, Cambridge University Press, 1970.

3 N. Frye, *The Secular Scripture*, Cambridge, Mass. and London, Harvard University Press, 1976.

4 For the influence of Greek romance on English literature, see especially S.L. Wolff, *The Greek Romances in Elizabethan Prose Fiction*, New York, Columbia University Press, 1912.

5 Good general accounts of the romances are given by B.E. Perry, *The Ancient Romances*, Berkeley and Los Angeles,

University of California Press, 1967 and T. Hägg, *The Novel in Antiquity*, Oxford, Basil Blackwell, 1983. Perry gives particular attention to the question of origins; Hägg explores some related literary types, such as travel tales and the romanticised lives of Christian saints, which I have not space to mention here. For a shorter account which includes the romance fragments, see also A. Lesky, *A History of Greek Literature*, London, Methuen, 1966, pp. 857–71. G. Anderson, in *Ancient Fiction: the Novel in the Graeco-Roman World*, London and Sydney, Croom Helm, 1984, explores the romances' oriental connections.

6 The translations from which I have quoted are the following. Chariton, *Chaereas and Callirhoe*, tr. W. Blake, London, Oxford University Press, 1939. Xenophon of Ephesus, 'An Ephesian tale', in *Three Greek Romances*, tr. M. Hadas, Indianapolis and New York, Bobbs-Merrill, 1953. Longus, 'Daphnis and Chloe', in the same volume. Achilles Tatius, *Clitophon and Leucippe*, tr. S. Gaselee, London, Heinemann, 1969. Heliodorus, *An Ethiopian Romance*, tr. M. Hadas, Ann Arbor, University of Michigan Press, 1957.

7 A. Carter, *The Sadeian Woman*, London, Virago, 1979.

8 For a brief account of tragedy from this point of view, see H. Foley, 'The conception of women in Athenian drama', in H. Foley, ed., *Reflections of Women in Antiquity*, New York, London and Paris, Gordon & Breach, 1981, especially pp. 148 ff.

9 On the link between the mode of performance of epic and Homer's ways of representing mental processes, see J. Russo and B. Simon, 'Homeric psychology and the oral epic tradition', in J. Wright, ed., *Essays on the Iliad*, Bloomington and London, Indiana University Press, 1978. The case of tragedy is complex in that it attempts increasingly to deal with the public-private split, but in the language of the public sphere. I have suggested that there is in Euripides an awareness of the limitations of tragic discourse for this purpose, in M. Williamson, 'A woman's place in Euripides' *Medea*', *JACT Review*, no. 3, Autumn 1985.

10 There is a growing literature on this subject. See S. Pomeroy, *Goddesses, Whores, Wives and Slaves*, London, Robert Hale, 1976, and the references in Foley (note 8 above).

11 For a detailed account of Longus' use of these traditions, see
   R.L. Hunter, *A Study of 'Daphnis and Chloe'*, Cambridge,
   Cambridge University Press, 1983.

Woodcut from Lloyd's Companion to *The Penny Sunday Times* and *People's Police Gazette*, 15 October 1843 (British Library)

3
The politics of seduction in English popular culture, 1748–1848

ANNA CLARK

In 1818, Birmingham audiences shaken by the real-life rape and murder of servant Mary Ashford could re-live the experience by watching a lurid melodrama entitled *The Murdered Maid*. They thrilled to see the villain 'Thornville' pursue the innocent 'Maria' as she cried, 'Begone, and learn that the humble and low-born Maria abhors the wretch, though a diadem sparkled on his brows, who would shock her ears with such base proposals and try to lure her from the paths of rectitude and honour.'[1] In the period of economic depression and political radicalism after the Napoleonic Wars, these strong words provided a clear, defiant metaphor of the exploitation of the poor by the upper classes.

As literary critics such as Martha Vicinus have noted, melodrama can be seen as a response to the traumas of the industrial revolution; its heroines, 'helpless and unbefriended', reflecting the feelings of loss of working class people faced with the destruction of traditional values.[2] In this article, I wish to build upon their insights to analyse the way in which the image of the poor maiden victimized by the aristocratic libertine provided a very specific symbol of class exploitation and explained familial traumas. Furthermore, this melodramatic image was explicitly political, becoming a crucial symbol in radical writing from the

47

Jacobins of the 1790s to the anti–Poor Law activists of the 1830s and 1840s.

In order to understand how the aristocratic libertine seducing the village maiden became such a pervasive metaphor in early nineteenth century working class culture, it is helpful to think of this image as a myth. A myth, as defined here, is a story which symbolically expresses anxieties brought about by social crisis. It provides people with an explanation for their inability to attain society's ideals in a time of disruptive change, and resolves their anxieties by redefining social norms.[3] The myth of seduction enabled fathers to blame familial crises on a predatory aristocracy while upholding chastity as an ideal. It portrayed class exploitation in vivid terms by presenting the theft of poor men's daughters by profligate aristocrats as a symbol for political exploitation and betrayal. As such, this image of seduction imbued fiction with a political content linking the reader to larger struggles, and inspired the public rhetoric of class struggle with personal, emotional images of oppression.

The rise of industrial capitalism engendered the crisis of the early nineteenth century working class. Paternalism became anachronistic in an era of bourgeois power; capitalist political economy rejected the obligation of the rich to the poor and replaced it with the cash nexus. For working people, capitalist modes of labour destroyed the old patriarchal family economy, in which the father controlled the labour power of his wife and children. And in times of economic crisis, traditional customs of common-law marriage and premarital pregnancy became problematic while female chastity became a requirement for respectable status.[4] In this context, the seduction and abandonment of the poor village girl by the wealthy squire could symbolize the betrayal of the working class by elite rulers. The myth of seduction also revealed the anguish of working fathers at losing their daughters' labour to exploitative employers, as well as the hardship of providing for illegitimate children.

Even as it expressed this economic and familial trauma, the myth of seduction was also mythical in the more ordinary sense of the term: it falsified reality, for class exploitation was exercised economically and politically, not sexually, while poor women faced sexual exploitation by men of their *own* class. Mary Ashford's real murderer was not a pedigreed rake but a local bricklayer named Abraham Thornton. The contrast between the sordid facts of the actual murder and its romantic, melodramatic incarnation is striking. In reality, very few unmarried mothers or victims of rape had fallen prey to aristocratic villains: the village lass was more likely to be seduced by a village lad than by the squire's son.[5]

Of course, the story of the aristocratic libertine and the poor village maiden could convey more meanings than the mythical one of class exploitation and familial trauma. On one hand, some men may have found the libertine's actions appealing in a sinister and erotic sense. On the other hand, some Gothic depictions of women fleeing aristocratic libertines could serve as a female fantasy of escape from sexual danger and oppressive families, especially in the late eighteenth century.[6] In this article I will concentrate on the class implications of the story. When seduction served as a myth of class exploitation, the seduced maiden became only a cipher in conflicts between men, rather than a heroine struggling to control her own destiny. Despite its power as a political metaphor, the myth muted female experience. It displaced potential anger at sexual exploitation to the level of class conflict, preventing working women from publicly articulating antagonism towards men of their own class.

The eighteenth century origins of the myth of seduction

The myth of seduction originated in the middle class genre of the novel. Sentimental novels, gothic novels, radical novels, all featured bourgeois heroines struggling with aristocratic villains. The virtue of the maiden illustrated bourgeois claims to moral and eventually political hegemony while the immorality of the aristocratic seducer shadowed his suitability to rule.[7]

Eighteenth century radicals rejected aristocratic paternalism. By refuting the claims of emotion and tradition with rational analysis, they exposed the gentry's claim of benevolent rule as fraudulent and corrupt. Henry Mackenzie illustrated the moral bankruptcy of the old ruling class in his novel *The Man of Feeling* by telling the story of the daughter of a half-pay officer 'reduced to squalid prostitution' by a squire's son.[8]

The most vivid radical attacks on the evils of aristocratic rule used the metaphor of incest to expose paternalism's fallacies.[9] As fathers were supposed to protect their daughters, noblemen were supposed to protect the poor; in the incest metaphor, fathers who raped their daughters symbolized rulers who exploit their subjects. Holcroft's play *The Deserted Daughter* describes a dissolute nobleman who abandons his illegitimate daughter and, twenty years later, unknowingly tries to seduce her, conveying a melodramatic attack on the aristocracy's moral impoverishment.[10] Similarly, Elizabeth Helme in *The Farmer of Inglewood Forest* portrays a West Indian plantation owner who upon his return to England almost rapes his long-lost daughter, his crime underlining her critique of slavery.[11]

By contrasting the inherent virtue of low-born heroines with the corruption of pedigreed seducers,

Jacobin novelists of the 1790s, such as Thomas Holcroft, William Godwin and Mary Wollstonecraft, also championed a just social order against Burke's organic hierarchy. They portrayed free-thinking women who took charge of their fates and escaped from the clutches of depraved aristocrats as well as repressive families. For them, the treatment meted out to unchaste women exemplified general social injustice as well as the oppression of women.[12]

In her novel *Maria, or the Wrongs of Women*, Mary Wollstonecraft depicts the sexual exploitation of a servant woman with a bitterness that mocks the sentimentality of typical novelistic seductions. The illegitimate daughter of a maidservant and a groom, Jemima is sent into service at a young age by a cruel stepmother. Her master repeatedly rapes her, and on discovery, her mistress throws her on to the streets, where she must turn to prostitution to survive. She tells the narrator, 'I have since read in novels of the blandishments of seduction, but I had not even the pleasure of being enticed into vice.'[13] Unlike most chroniclers of fictional seduction, Wollstonecraft never confused consensual sex with rape. In most discourses about seduction, this distinction was not important, for the loss of female chastity, rather than violence, gave these stories their tragic point.

By the end of the 1790s, however, the bourgeois reaction against the French Revolution effectively silenced attacks on conventional morals by attributing its excesses to sexual freedom as well as political radicalism. Mary Wollstonecraft herself was long reviled for her sexual affairs.

The myth of seduction as a nineteenth century political metaphor

As Gareth Stedman Jones has shown, radical discourses

of the 1790s retained their power through the 1840s despite dramatically different political and class configurations.[14] Even as it lost its sexual daring, the myth of seduction did gain strength as a class metaphor. Its political significance, however, became transformed by the struggles of the nascent working class. The seduced maiden and the libertine began to represent the working class against capitalists, as well as the bourgeoisie against the aristocracy. The myth's emotional tenor changed; while Jacobin versions stressed the heroine's defiance of patriarchal norms in favour of Utopian freedom, early nineteenth century versions emphasized her father's grief and anxiety, her fall symbolizing the perceived loss of a past golden age.[15] Popular literature expressed these traumas in fictional form; political rhetoric eventually incorporated this metaphor as an explicit illustration of class exploitation which aroused an emotional recognition from working class audiences. By linking personal tragedies with politics, this myth provided an interpretive framework which could be found in fiction, newspaper reportage and radical rhetoric.

The myth of seduction spread from three-decker novels appealing to prosperous readers into the burgeoning popular press. Innovations in printing and increased literacy in the first decades of the nineteenth century led to a flood of ballads, chapbooks and, by the 1830s, penny-issue novels, all of which appealed to working people.[16] The story of the poor village maiden and the aristocratic libertine could be told on the single sheet of a ballad sung in the streets, embellished into the endless plot of a penny-issue novel, or enacted on the stage of a plebeian theatre as a thrilling melodrama. While these plays and novels were often directly adopted from the works by eighteenth century radicals,[17] their sensibility differed from the Jacobin stress on reason; it was the sensibility of melodrama.

Melodrama appealed to all classes of society, even the poorest, easily adapting itself to an inchoate popular politics. Its action typically moved between fantastical scenes of high life and ultra-realistic depictions of low life in an atmosphere of suspense and heightened emotion. Audiences could both identify with their characters' woes and escape through theatrical exoticism. As Peter Brooks writes,

> Melodrama starts from and expresses the anxiety brought by a frightening new world in which the traditional patterns of moral order no longer provide the necessary social glue. It plays out the force of that anxiety with the apparent triumph of villainy, and it dissipates it with the eventual victory of virtue.[18]

As Vicinus notes, melodrama derived especial resonance from its expression of the 'conflict between the family and its values and the economic and social assault of industrialization'.[19] But it was also a recognition of the fact that traditional family values were in flux. The introduction of the capitalist division of labour into industries such as textile production, shoemaking, tailoring, and so on undermined the family economy. Male artisans found that mechanization and the low-paid labour of women and children often displaced their hard-won skills. Repeated depressions also robbed many working men of jobs, forcing them to wander far from home in search of wages. This economic uncertainty undermined traditional courtship patterns of premarital sex and even stable cohabitation; working women would enter sexual relationships expecting their lovers would marry them or at least support a household, only to find themselves abandoned and pregnant. As a result, illegitimacy rates rocketed; the bastardy clauses, intended to prevent illicit pregnancies, only exacerbated the problems of unmarried mothers.[20]

In response to this social disruption, some working class people strove to attain a respectable status, often defined as the male worker's ability to support his wife and children, and the chastity of female members of the family. The seduction of a daughter by an irresponsible young man could be the blow that crumbled a father's hard-won reputation. By blaming illegitimacy on the depradations of aristocratic libertines, melodrama provided a symbolic explanation for the failure of fathers to attain respectability.

The patriarchal version of the myth of seduction had such great appeal because it echoed deeply felt sentiments. Petitions to the London Foundling Hospital often contained letters from fathers imploring that institution to accept their daughters' bastard children in order to save their own honour. While the circumstances may have induced them to exaggerate, they described their grief in greater detail than their daughters' plights. For instance, a Clerkenwell operative mechanic scrawled in an uncertain hand, 'I just confess the shock of this affair has given as nearly deprived me of the ability of attending to what little work I can get [sic].' A 'respectable' Leicestershire father wrote of 'this heavy calamity which has bowed me and my wife nearly down to the grave'. Mr Johns, a bailiff, became broken-hearted when his labourer impregnated his daughter, and turned her out of the house.[21]

The grief of fathers at their daughters' seduction provided a central emotional dynamic in melodramatic plots. Mrs Opie's *Father and Daughter* and more popular imitators such as T.P. Prest's *The Maniac Father, or The Victim of Seduction* featured fathers stricken by bankruptcy and madness after the noble villains enticed away their daughters.[22] They stressed the moralistic lesson that misbehaving daughters betrayed their fathers, with horrible consequences for their families and themselves.

Fictional upper class villains could be blamed for more specific oppressions. The factory owner raping the working girl symbolized industry's disruption of the household economy and its destruction of the patriarchal artisan's skill and authority. Young men provided the fourth character in the structure of conflict between father, daughter, and villain, replacing paternal impotence with youthful vigour in defying oppression. In *The Factory Lad*, the pauper Sally becomes 'the unyielding, resisting victim of a monster's lust', the villain being Thorneycroft, a 'heartless cotton lord'. In revenge for her ruin and his own exploitation in the mill, Sally's brother vows to blow up the factory but instead faces humiliation by Thorneycroft's henchmen.[23]

Absentee landlords and their wicked stewards also aroused popular ire, reflecting the insecurity of small farmers racked by agricultural depression and the increasing intrusion of capitalism. A short story from a radical Sunday newspaper of the 1840s, 'The squire, or The farmer's daughter', illustrated these motifs. Realistically depicting Farmer Wood's woes – rheumatic fever, the death of two children, and the loss of his corn and cattle – the story employs the myth of seduction to underscore agricultural oppression. His landlord's steward offers to excuse his debt in return for the hand of Farmer Wood's daughter. Unwilling to sacrifice herself to the steward, pretty young Mary seeks help from the squire, but this 'extravagant young man' drunkenly 'attempts to seize her in his arms' instead of listening to her pleas. Fortunately, stalwart young William Ashton overhears 'the whole of the discourse with a flushed cheek and kindling anger' and rescues Mary, knocking the squire to the ground.[24]

Despite their radical vigour, both these stories clearly portray women as pawns in struggles between men.

Another young hero who defies aristocratic libertines appears in T.P. Prest's *Emily Fitzormond* (1842), which appeared both as a novel and as a melodrama. When Sir Edgecumbe Sappington and Captain Bellingham, two officers fond of military flogging, attempt to abduct the novel's heroines, manly young Henry Walton, a farmer's son, foils their plan, declaring, 'Desist! Remember, as stout a heart often beats beneath a peasant's humble jacket, as an officer's gold-laced coat, and unprovoked insolence may make that heart doubly resolute.' In retaliation, the villains arrange with a magistrate to have Henry press-ganged.[25]

Radical fictions had long portrayed such aristocratic seducers corrupting British justice to their own ends as symptomatic of the system's inherent class bias. In Elizabeth Inchbald's popular novel *Nature and Art*, William, the son of a wealthy notable, seduces and abandons Agnes, a village lass. Agnes flees to the city where poverty soon drives her to prostitution and theft. In a dramatic denouement, she is brought to trial before William, now a judge, who sentences her to death for forgery without recognizing her.[26] The novelette *Innocence Betrayed* includes another such story: Maria Thornhill is lured into prostitution and deserted by her seducer. He becomes a wealthy magistrate who refuses her aid when she is reduced to begging for her food.[27]

The myth of seduction gained such a powerful emotional credibility from these fictions that it actually shaped and distorted people's perceptions of real sexual exploiters of women. Violent crimes could be transformed into melodramatic myths. The controversy over Abraham Thornton and Mary Ashford, for instance, provided fodder not only for newspaper reporters and lurid pamphlets but also for at least three plays and many ballads. As we have seen, Mary Ashford, a servant, had been raped and murdered by a bricklayer, Abraham Thornton, but he was acquitted of both crimes. After the trial, a reporter noted, 'Among the lower classes of people about the neighbourhood, there is a sense of horror against Thornton, that amounts almost to ferocity; and this is accompanied by a most indecorous and general outcry against all the means which led to his dismissal.'[28] Melodramatic depictions of the crime in plays and ballads attributed Thornton's acquittal to his ability to bribe the jury with his father's supposed wealth. The melodramas about Mary Ashford also linked this injustice with the sufferings of working people under the agricultural depression following the Napoleonic Wars. Yet by depicting Thornton's crime as a symptom of aristocratic oppression, these melodramas concealed the murder's disturbing implications for sexual relations between working men and women. Mary Ashford was portrayed as a heroine who died defending her chastity against a noble villain, not as a woman who followed traditional courtship customs only to be assaulted by a man of her own class.

In another example of the power of the myth of seduction to evade the reality of sexual assault within the working class, London newspapers during the early nineteenth century often featured reports of 'fashionable young men' harassing 'respectable married females' on the street. The radical *Weekly Dispatch* melodramatically compared such 'gentlemen of fashion' to the aristocrats Waldegrave and Waterford who were fined token amounts for similar 'outrageous assaults'.

> What is the conclusion? That any of the Waterfordists, or Waldegravites, may seize any poor man's, tradesman's, or respectable gentleman's wife, sister

or daughter round the waist in the open streets,
throw her on the ground in a violent manner, fall
upon her, ruin her bonnet and her dress, deprive her
of her parasol, may knock down her companion,
whether it be her husband, father, brother, friend, or
lover, brutally beat him as he lies senseless, all for
the paltry price of a few pounds. The bosom swells
with disgust and indignation at such a decision.

This language clearly echoes the fictional frustration of
the factory lad, Henry Walton or William Ashton
when faced with upper class young men who could
assault them and their women with impunity from the
law. Its fictional origins become even more apparent
when we discover that the 'gentlemen of fashion' the
above quote alluded to were actually one journeyman
carpenter and one resident of the distinctly unfashion-
able neighbourhood of Soho.[29] The myth of seduction
was so powerful it concealed the reality that libertinism
transcended class boundaries.

The politics of seduction

The melodramatic evasion of the realities of working
class sexual violence, however, allowed the myth of
seduction to gain added political force. By portraying
the aristocratic libertine as the sole cause of the seduced
maiden's fall, melodrama claimed morality as a working
class prerogative. While Utilitarians and Evangelicals
placed the blame for illegitimacy and familial distin-
tegration on the moral flaws of the poor, radicals
accused the rich of sexual and economic profligacy;
they portrayed illegitimacy and familial disruption
symbolically as tragedies caused not by personal
inadequacy but by class exploitation.

Radical political rhetoric incorporated both the
themes and styles of melodrama.[30] Melodrama

abandoned bourgeois novels' subtle explorations of inner states for a black and white division of good and evil, which easily transferred to an identification of political foes and allies.

Instead of the cool reason of Godwin, early nineteenth century Radicals drew upon the fierce biblical language of Dissenting religion, portraying the epitome of virtue as the starving working man's family and the nadir of vice as the corrupt, exploitative nobility. Cobbett's great motif was the betrayal of the poor by the rich – he desired a paternalism which he knew no longer existed, and this is what inspired his vigorous rage. The seduced maiden paralleled the honest working man who had trusted his betters only to be exploited by them. Once, Cobbett declared, England had been populated by happy, free, yeoman families in villages ruled by benevolent squires. Now, the excesses of the Regency Court – the dandyism, the hundreds of thousands of pounds spent in gambling and extravagant entertaining – provided living examples of profligate blue-bloods squandering the nation's wealth while the people suffered from war and depression.

The myth of seduction explicitly entered political discourse in the anti-Poor Law movement of the 1830s and 1840s, for the debate over the Poor Laws centred around a Utilitarian attack on working-class families' legitimacy and counter-accusations of sexual exploitation. Its use in this rhetoric represented a continuity with radical rhetoric from the 1790s and enabled middle and working class opponents of the bastardy clauses to find common ground on a defence of female purity. Replacing the old system of locally administered relief, the repressive New Poor Law mandated the incarceration of the poor in austere workhouses. Furthermore, the New Poor Law's bastardy clauses exonerated men from their previous responsibility to maintain their illegitimate children, forcing unmarried mothers to seek shelter in the punitive workhouses. The 1834 Report on the Poor Laws clearly reveals its writers' fear of poor women's sexuality, describing them as 'shameless and unprincipled'.[31]

Working people interpreted these insinuations as an insult to their integrity and an encouragement to male immorality. While the New Poor Law's harsh measures and its rejection of paternalism inspired a militant anti-Poor Law movement, the bastardy clauses were even more unpopular among a large and diverse sector of public opinion.

Radicals described the bastardy clauses as an aristo-cratic plot to ease the seduction of poor women. At a large Bradford anti-Poor Law meeting, Peter Bussey denounced the upper class exploitation of poor men's labour, declaring,

> There is a set of young boobies in this country, who are connected with the aristocracy, and who are regular plunderers of the people; they seek your blood, they would weaken your sinews, and they would destroy your lives; but you are useful in labouring for them.

He went on to link economic with sexual domination:

> This brood are on the increase, and they are in the habit of seducing the daughters of poor men, and I have formed an opinion that the bastardy clauses have been introduced into this act, in order to protect, and to screen the despicable aristocrat in all his wicked intrigues [hear hear] or even to murder the offspring of those who are the object of his seducing snares.[32]

Opponents of the bastardy clauses tied its exoneration

of men from responsibility with the excesses of the market economy. The *Morning Herald* reviled the clauses' 'more than Turkish contempt for the claims of betrayed and suffering woman on the profligate seducer, who may now hug his golden god in security, while he spurns his imploring victim and their common offspring with his feet!'[33]

Such florid rhetoric defended unmarried mothers by characterizing them as innocent, helpless and asexual. In contrast to this stereotype, working class women themselves vigorously protested against every aspect of the New Poor Law, rioting against Poor Law Commissioners, attending torch-light meetings on moors, and meeting in large numbers to send Parliament petitions expressing opposition to the law. They attacked the bastardy clauses's unfairness to their daughters and asserted their right as women to protest.[34]

And by portraying the seduced maiden as a passive victim of upper class profligacy, the myth of seduction also contributed to a wider rhetoric of the poor as weak and passive victims who needed to be protected by kindly paternalists. Some upper class paternalists did participate in the anti-Poor Law movement, resenting the new law's tendency to usurp their local influence. But they lacked the political power to defeat the New Poor Law itself. By the late 1830s and 1840s, working class agitators, furthermore, began to realize that the miseries of the Industrial Revolution could not be ameliorated by benevolent landowners and factory owners. They did not want to be treated like helpless children by Tory radicals; they rejected such leaders as Oastler when he refused to support universal 'manhood' suffrage.

Despite women's political vigour, the eagerness of working class men to repudiate paternalism was often accompanied by enthusiasm for a patriarchal politics of gender. As part of their demand for political manhood, working class men (save for Owenites) claimed the privileges of the middle-class Victorian patriarch, and this meant they wished to be heads of their own households and support their own wives. A typical articulation of this patriarchal demand, so frequently found in contemporary radical rhetoric, is the following speech by anti-Poor Law leader Rev. J.R. Stephens. A large crowd enthusiastically responded when he declared:

> God cursed woman as well as man . . . that she should be in subjection to her own husband, her desire should be unto her husband, and he should rule over her [hear hear] and not the millowners [tremendous cheering] — not the coal pit master [continued cheering] — not the Poor Law Commissioners.[35]

While Parliament would not grant universal manhood suffrage, it responded more sympathetically to working class men's demands for patriarchal protection of women and children. The bastardy clauses offended many middle class people as immoral and Poor Law officials themselves criticized it as unworkable; as a result, the clauses were modified in 1844, allowing unmarried mothers an expensive and inconvenient method of attaining redress from their seducers. The parliamentary restriction of women's work in the factories and mines stemmed from a patriarchal belief, shared by both upper class and working class men, that women were passive and weak victims who required protection.

Conclusion – the limitations of the myth of seduction

Despite its utility in political rhetoric, the radical implications of the myth of seduction were quite limited: it was a defensive weapon in a discursive combat whose arena was determined by the bourgeois value of chastity. It accepted the notion that seduction was the worst thing that could happen to a woman, but blamed the upper class for this phenomenon. Rejecting the sexual radicalism of the eighteenth century, the myth spoke to the fears of fathers, brothers and lovers rather than women themselves.

The myth of seduction distorted the realities of working class life not only by evading the reality of rape committed by poor men, but by failing to defend the validity of courtship customs encompassing pre-marital sex and common-law unions. These extralegal relationships became a problem only when economic disruption made them unstable, when unemployment made it more likely that men would desert their pregnant lovers or that mothers would have to bring up children alone.

There was an alternative discourse at this time which illuminated these courtship traditions with political relevance: it was developed by the Owenite socialists, who proclaimed the value of free love, socialist unions between the sexes, and the equality of women. They also refused to consider women's sexuality as a form of property. As Barbara Taylor has shown, however, Owenite men and women saw these values quite differently. The Owenite critique of chastity foundered on its inability to acknowledge the material roots of sexual antagonism within the working class. Owenite women hesitated to endorse the sexual freedom their male comrades so enthusiastically sought. A tenuous economic position, not to speak of sexual violence, prevented many working class women from regarding sexual pleasure as their primary goal. In a time of economic depression, a woman's chastity was indeed her most precious possession and marriage necessary for survival.[36] Owenite men refused to acknowledge the complicity of working class men in the sexual exploitation of working class women. As one socialist declared, the bastardy clauses were introduced to 'screen a vile aristocracy, who seduce and ruin more young girls than all the other male population put together'.[37]

Barbara Taylor has astutely pointed out that the repudiation of the Owenites' call for a transformation of gender as well as class relations led to a narrow trade-union politics dominated by the male labour aristocracy. Such a conception of politics also led to the decline of working class women's previously vigorous political role.[38]

In the late 1830s and 1840s, fictional portrayals of seduced maidens began to mirror this trend. While radical fiction attributed women's fall to poverty and injustice, its seduced heroines almost always died in implicit atonement for their shame. As Sally Mitchell notes, such stories thus expressed 'the emotional tension of the woman who perceives wrongs – both socially and in her own position – but is absolutely without power . . . man may alter events; woman is simply acted upon'.[39]

The meaning of a popular text derives from complex negotiations with its audience. As we have seen, the myth of seduction derived from eighteenth century texts but acquired new meaning in the context of the sexual crisis of the early nineteenth century working class. It expressed anxiety over the social and political turmoil of the early nineteenth century, linking personal with structural crises. Displacing possible female anger over sexual exploitation within the working class, it attributed the uncertainties of working class family formation to the depradations of aristocratic villains. As a symbol for class exploitation in political rhetoric, it was structured by patriarchal assumptions rather than a Utopian search for female freedom from sexual danger. The maiden in distress could only be rescued by the stalwart working man; despite the bold activism of working class women, they were little represented in radical iconography. The sexual conservatism of the political rhetoric derived in turn from the personal solution to familial trauma adopted as an ideal (but rarely attained) by many working class people: the ideology of separate spheres and the family wage.

Whatever its limitations, the power of the myth of seduction illuminates the politics of popular literature. First, it shows how one theme, the seduced maiden, and one sensibility, melodrama, could pervade the genres of crime reporting, novels, theatre and political rhetoric. Second, it was not an image manipulated from above, but one which appealed to a popular audience not only because it explained personal and political traumas but because it was entertaining and moving. Finally, it reveals a symbiotic relationship between popular fiction and popular politics: the existence of working-class struggle imbued fiction with political meaning, and the fictional myth of seduction gave radical rhetoric a rare emotional depth.

Acknowledgments

Many people have made helpful suggestions about this paper in its evolution from part of my MA thesis at the University of Essex. I would first like to thank Leonore Davidoff for her guidance and the inspiration of her own work; Raphael Samuel also helped me develop my ideas and provided references. At Rutgers

University, Judith Walkowitz, John Gillis and Suzanne Lebsock have aided in revising the paper. Most of all, my friends from the London Feminist History Group – especially Deborah Mabbett and Alison Oram – and the Rutgers women's history seminar – Laura Tabili, Polly Beals, Carolyn Strange, Adrienne Scerbak and Claudia Clark – have provided me with continuous support and encouragement.

Notes

1 S.N.E. [George Ludlam], *The Murdered Maid* (Warwick, 1818), pp. 12–13.

2 Martha Vicinus, 'Helpless and unbefriended: 19th century domestic melodrama', *New Literary History*, vol. XIII, no. 1 (Autumn 1981), p. 143.

3 This definition of myth is derived from readings in Claude Lévi-Strauss, *The Savage Mind* (London: Weidenfeld & Nicolson, 1966), pp. 68–9; Mary Douglas, *Implicit Meanings: Essays in Anthropology* (London: Routledge & Kegan Paul, 1966), p. 156; and Carroll Smith-Rosenberg, 'Davey Crockett as trickster: pornography, liminality, and symbolic inversion in Victorian America', *Journal of Contemporary History*, vol. V, no. 17 (1982), p. 325; see also Judith R. Walkowitz's use of myth in her 'Jack the Ripper and the myth of male violence', *Feminist Studies*, Fall 1982–3.

4 Lawrence Stone, *The Family, Sex and Marriage*, abridged version (New York: Harper, 1979), pp. 410–18. David Levine, *Family Formation in an Age of Nascent Capitalism* (New York: Academic Press, 1972), p. 137. John Gillis, *For Better, For Worse: A Political and Social History of British Marriage* (Oxford: Oxford University Press, 1986).

5 John R. Gillis, 'Servants, sexual relations, and the risks of illegitimacy in London, 1801–1900', *Feminist Studies*, vol. V, no. 1 (Spring 1979), p. 158. See also Anna Clark, *Women's Silence, Men's Violence: Sexual Assault in England 1770–1845*, London, Pandora Press, 1986.

6 For the story of seduction as a male fantasy, Richardson and Lewis portrayed the rapists' arousal. See Samuel Richardson,

Clarissa (San Francisco: Rinehart Press, 1971, abridged edition) and M.G. Lewis, *The Monk: A Romance* (London: Oxford University Press, 1973). Rosemary Jackson discusses this in her book *Fantasy: The Literature of Subversion* (London: Methuen, 1981).

For the female fantasy of escape from rape, see Judith Lowder Newton, *Women, Power and Subversion* (Athens, Georgia: University of Georgia Press, 1981); Katherine Ellis, 'Charlotte Smith's subversive gothic', *Feminist Studies*, vol. 3, no. 3/4 (Spring/Summer 1976), p. 55; Coral Ann Howells, *Love, Mystery, and Misery: Feeling in Gothic Fiction* (London: Athlone Press, 1978). For the origins of the tradition of female heroism in middle class novels, see Donna Lee Weber, 'Fair game: rape and sexual aggression in some early 18th century prose' (University of Toronto, PhD, 1980), pp. 154, 212. There was also a plebeian tradition of female heroism in escaping rape: see such ballads as 'Undaunted Mary' or 'The Squire and the Milkmaid' in the Baring-Gould Collection of Ballads, British Library, London.

7 Marilyn Butler, *Jane Austen and the War of Ideas* (Oxford: Clarendon Press, 1975), pp. 29–50, discusses the political implications of these novels. See also Gary Kelly, *The English Jacobin Novel* (Oxford: Clarendon Press, 1976), pp. 17, 30.

8 Butler, op.cit., p. 104.

9 Peter Thorsler, 'Incest as a romantic symbol', *Comparative Literature Studies* II (1965), pp. 42–7. Predatory, incestuous father figures are also, of course, a theme which must have drawn upon women's fears of real incest and of protectors who turned out to be sexually exploitative. For an example of an aged aristocratic roué pursuing the heroine and being unmasked as her father, see the anonymous popular novel *Seduction* (London, 1848). For an example of an incestuous uncle, see M.G. Lewis, *The Castle Spectre* in Lacy's Acting Edition, vol. XV. For a novel concerning pursuit by a father figure, the father of the heroine's lover, see Anonymous, *The Adventures of Sylvia Hughes* (New York: Garland, 1975 (1761)). In T.P. Prest's *Emily Fitzormond* (London, 1842) the orphan heroine fears that her mysterious, aged and lascivious guardian is her father: '. . . perhaps that wretch, that miscreant, was her father? . . . Was it possible that the hoary-headed man, who affected so

much kindness and benevolence, should contemplate the violation of a poor, deserted, friendless, girl, to whom he was old enough to be a grandfather?' (pp. 140–1).

10 Thomas Holcroft, 'The deserted daughter', in *The Acting Drama*, (London, 1834), p. 55.

11 Elizabeth Helme, *The Farmer of Inglewood Forest* (London, 1796).

12 Butler, op.cit., pp. 43–50.

13 Mary Wollstonecraft, *Maria, or the Wrongs of Woman* (Oxford: Oxford University Press, 1980), p. 109.

14 Gareth Stedman Jones, 'Rethinking Chartism', in his *Languages of Class: Studies in English Working Class History 1832–1982* (Cambridge: Cambridge University Press, 1983), p. 102.

15 Susan Staves, in her 'British seduced maidens', *Eighteenth Century Studies*, vol. XIV, no. 2 (Winter 1980/1), pp. 42–55, emphasizes the conservative versions of the story of seduction in the eighteenth century which stress the father's grief.

16 Louis James, *Print and the People, 1819–1851* (Harmondsworth: Penguin, 1978), pp. 1–20. See also his *Fiction for the Working Man* (Harmondsworth: Penguin, 1974); James C. Smith, *Victorian Melodrama* (London: Dent, 1976); R.K. Webb, *The British Working Class Reader* (London: Allen & Unwin, 1955); and A.P. Wadsworth, 'Newspaper circulations 1800–1854', *Transactions of the Manchester Statistical Society* (March 1955), p. 12.

17 The influence of fiction on popular theatre can be seen in the case of eighteenth century novels which were republished in popular versions in the early nineteenth century and then transformed into melodramas. For example, Elizabeth Helme's *The Farmer of Inglewood Forest* was originally published in London in 1796 and republished there in 1822 and 1824. In 1846 it was made into a melodrama by W. Rogers (British Museum Add. MS. 42991ff.678–722).

18 Peter Brooks, *The Melodramatic Imagination* (New Haven and London: Yale University Press, 1976), p. 44.

19 Vicinus, op.cit., p. 128.

20 Barbara Taylor, *Eve and the New Jerusalem: Socialism and Feminism in the 19th Century* (New York: Pantheon, 1983), pp. 213 ff.

21 Foundling Hospital Petitions 1838-ac-166; 1818-rej.-unn. (S.H.); 1826-ac-21; 1844-rej-195; 1842-rej-181. All names have been

changed in accordance with archival regulations.

22 Mrs Amelia Opie, *The Father and Daughter* (London, 1802); T.P. Prest, *The Maniac Father, or The Victim of Seduction* (London, 1844).

23 James, *Print and the People*, pp. 116–17.

24 *Lloyd's Companion to the Penny Sunday Times and People's Police Gazette*, 15 October 1843. Douglas Jerrold's *The Rent Day* (in *British Plays of the 19th Century*, ed. Jo Bailey (New York: Odyssey Press, 1966), first performed in 1832, followed a similar theme.

25 T.P. Prest, *Emily Fitzormond* (London, 1842), pp. 142 ff. To be 'press-ganged' means to be abducted by groups of men authorized by the government to impress young men into the navy against their will.

26 Elizabeth Inchbald, *Nature and Art* (London, 1796).

27 Anonymous, *Innocence Betrayed, or Infamy Avowed, Being the History of Miss Maria Thornhill* (Manchester, 1810).

28 *Horrible Rape and Murder! The Affecting Case of Mary Ashford . . .* (London, 1817), p 51; S.N.E., op.cit., *The Mysterious Murder* (Birmingham, ca. 1818). For a further discussion of this case, see my book cited above and the article 'Rape or seduction?' in London Feminist History Group, ed., *The Sexual Dynamics of History* (London: Pluto Press, 1982).

29 *Weekly Dispatch*, 2,9,and 15 August 1840.

30 I would like to thank Raphael Samuel for this insight.

31 Great Britain Commissioners for Inquiry, *Report into the Administration and Practical Operation of the Poor Laws* (London, 1834), p. 350.

32 From an unlabelled newspaper clipping in the Francis Place Collection, British Museum, vol. 56. Anti-Poor Law meeting at Bradford.

33 Quoted in *Nottingham Journal*, 15 August 1834.

34 *Nottingham Journal*, 28 July 1837, *London Dispatch*, 11 March 1838, 25 February 1838; *Northern Star*, 3 February, 24 February 1838.

35 G.R. Wythen Baxter, *The Book of the Bastiles, or The History of the Workings of the New Poor Law* (London, 1841), p. 398.

36 Taylor, op.cit., p. 213 ff.

37 Allen Davenport, *Life of Thomas Spence* (1839), p. 22, quoted in Judith R. Walkowitz, *Prostitution and Victorian Society* (Cambridge:

Cambridge University Press, 1980), p. 35.

38 Dorothy Thompson, 'Women and radical politics: a lost dimension', in *The Rights and Wrongs of woman*, ed. Juliet Mitchell and Ann Oakley (Harmondsworth: Penguin, 1976), p. 125; Taylor, op.cit., p. 273.

39 Sally Mitchell, 'The forgotten female of the period: penny weekly family magazines of the 1830s and 1840s', in *A Widening Sphere*, ed. Martha Vicinus (Bloomington, Ind.: Indiana University Press, 1978), p. 43.

Whitworth Collieries, Tredegar (by kind permission of John Cornwell, Mining Photographer)

4

How Green Was My Valley:
a romance of Wales

DERRICK PRICE

Many Welsh critics have given *How Green Was My Valley* a hard time. They have attacked it for its lack of verisimilitude to working class life; for its obfuscation and reactionary analysis of significant historical struggles; for its individualist account of political action; and for its racism and sentimentality. In this article I do not set out to rescue Richard Llewellyn's book from these well-founded critical judgments. But I do stand with those critics who see it as an interesting, complex, and even a key text in the body of writing about the industrial valleys of South Wales.[1]

What most obviously marks the book out for special attention is its awe-inspiring popularity. It can be read in more than a dozen languages and its international readership is numbered in many millions. Nor was the book a triumph abroad but scorned at home. If it returned to the people of the mining valleys a bizarre and inaccurate picture of themselves, it was certainly one that they embraced with pleasure; whether they read it on the pages of the book or saw it on the screen in John Ford's movie version.

Ford's was not the only feature film to be made about industrial South Wales; for some years before it appeared in 1941 there had been a great deal of interest in the area. Together with Hollywood movies there were many documentary films, a great deal of reportage, and a small but significant stream of literary production by working class writers. The best known of these are the novels of Jack Jones, Gwyn Jones and Lewis Jones together with the autobiographical writing of B.L. Coombes. From one standpoint these writers can be seen as fitting into a pattern of activity which was typical of the 1930s, and regarded as part of a general 'movement' of working class writing which took place throughout Britain. From another point of view, though, they are very special because, before the 1930s, very few Anglo-Welsh writers had taken the communities of the valleys as their subject matter.[2] The novels of the 1930s are centrally concerned with the material circumstances that bear down on their characters, who are living lives of quiet crisis or active struggle. Their writing is, then, about work and unemployment; about the fight of families to overcome hardship and want. They are also about the solidarity of community life and the pleasures of communal activity. And these families and communities are represented to us as drawn from, and exemplary of, existing families and communities.

At the superficial level of 'themes' *How Green Was My Valley* might be seen as fitting neatly enough into this kind of writing. It is a novel about the life of a working class family and is concerned with work, religion, strikes, music, rugby, etc. All Welsh life is there! But, as soon as we begin to read the book, we realise that we are in a very different territory.

> I am going to pack my two shirts with my other socks and my best suit in the little blue cloth my mother used to tie round her hair when she did the house, and I am going from the Valley.

These famous lines[3] set the tone of the book and within a few pages it becomes clear that we are not reading a realist novel. The text is organised by the use of nostalgia and sentimentality to give us an account of life in the valleys in which history, memory and political action are stripped of collectivity and presented as the qualities of heroic individuals. But, no matter what critical distance we choose to maintain, many of us have also been hooked. It is possible to give up reading the book later, when the episodic style, the looseness of construction, and the piling on of incident begin to jar and irritate. For the moment, though, we are in thrall to Huw Morgan's retrospective account of the life of the valley he is imminently going to leave. We will find out later that the events he is describing all happened 'thirty years ago', but this precise dating is of little importance because the past to which we are introduced – although it draws on events of the time – has no real historical location. Instead, we are taken to a mythic past and invited to share Huw's early recollections of life in the Morgan family.

These are firstly memories of pleasure; of gargantuan wholesome meals and of a child's warm security as he sits on his mother's lap among the smells and tastes and familial communality of Saturday dinner (the family's Nonconformist religion proscribes cooking on Sundays). Oral gratifications are important throughout the book but they are always accompanied by an account of the pattern of life that made them possible. All the food and toffees and treats of Huw's childhood have been paid for in sovereigns and his personal golden past is, we are told, typical of the richness of the community in which he lives. But we have to read this in the knowledge that the golden age is over, for he often interrupts his reminiscences to point up the comparison between past pleasures and the bleakness of the present:

It makes you think of so much that was good that

has gone. But when we used to sit down to
dinner . . . it was lovely to look at the table. Mind,
in those days, nobody thought of looking at the
table to keep the memory of it living in their minds.
(p.10)

Since this is a book of reminiscences, it is useful to
consider what kind of memory it deals with. The
working class novels of the 1930s are crucially
concerned with a re-working of popular memory and
communally determined accounts of the past. Written
in the years after 1926 – a time of workers' defeats –
they explore the nature of the contemporary crisis,
both by describing how it felt to live through it, and
by interrogating the past in order to analyse its causes.
'Memory', in these texts, is personal, communal and
social.

Although *How Green Was My Valley* was published
in 1939, it does not directly address the 1930s at all.
But through the apparently individual and random
memories of its narrator it does offer us a highly
charged account of the problems of that decade. Like
many other romances, the book depends for its power
on its construction of the past as irrevocably ruptured
from the present. The past is not mobilised in the
service of recuperating or illuminating the present and
the future. Rather, it is treated as a site of tranquillity,
order and apparent permanence. A place of unproblematic relationships and time-hallowed ways of
doing things; a place, that is, outside history – a place
of nature.

What makes this particularly interesting, and provides
How Green Was My Valley with its power as a text, is
that Wales has, for several hundred years, precisely
been seen as a site of nature. And while *How Green
Was My Valley* has usually been compared with the
novels of industrial life, it is useful to see it as deriving

much of its form and its view of Wales from the travel books and romances of the nineteenth century. The Wales of these books excludes the industrial valleys of the South, and concentrates on rural areas somewhere in the hills of the South-west and North. Here, Wales is seen as a peaceful place, remote and beautiful. As Anne Beale put it in 1844:

> When I came hither, a stranger, I was struck by the loneliness of the country, as well as by the character, manners and language of its primitive inhabitants. . . . There are many who delight to fly from the noise and hustle of the world to regions of seclusion and peace, where they can look upon Nature as she came fresh from the hand of her Maker, and find in her children something of their original simplicity and purity.[4]

Immediately before this passage, Anne Beale observes that people will expect some account of the 'agrarian excitement' lately spread through South Wales. But she had finished her book before 'our tranquil vales and mountains witnessed the outbreaks of a disease which I hope is now cured and became scenes of civil warfare and midnight violence'.[5]

The book itself contains no hint that the simple people of the rural Wales she invokes were about to burst into the Rebecca Riots. Instead, she draws on that Wales which was used as a source of inspiration for the construction of theories of the picturesque in the eighteenth century. By the time Frances Burnett wrote *Miss Crespigny* in 1878 it was enough merely to use the word 'picturesque' in order to conjure up Wales:

> During a summer visit to a quaint, picturesque village on the Welsh coast, she had made the

acquaintance of the owners of a quaint, picturesque cottage, whose picturesqueness had taken her fancy.[6]

Quite. And with a few such touches the Welshness of her text is established and the novel proceeds with no direct encounter with any aspect of the country or people.

The Welsh themselves are in this writing seen as simple, idle, innocent and pure. Indeed, Bertha Thomas, who bicycled to Wales in 1899, tells us archly that:

> It is my firm belief – corroborated by the most recent prehistoric research – that the original Pixyland was in Wales. The landsmen – the little men, the tricky men, the unaccountable, elusive, secret people of the hills – mighty for mischief, or for kindness, according as they choose – dark, quaint headed, quaintly clad – you may call them Welsh, or Picts, or Ibero-Silurian, or the ten tribes, or what you please – I call them Pixies.[7]

This would be merely silly if it did not, in an extreme form, represent a way of seeing Wales and the Welsh that has a long history and helped to create an English readership for stories of romance set in the hills of Wales. The most popular and successful of writers of romances with Welsh settings and characters was Allen Raine whose books sold millions of copies. Sally Jones points out in her study of Raine that she wove into her romances a great deal of insider's knowledge about the life and work of the people of her part of Wales.[8] Unlike the tourists, she was concerned with the hard features of the countryside, as well as with exploring its romantic possibilities.

Richard Llewellyn's romance also draws on a real history and employs features of the life of the valleys.

In the early years of their industrialisation they were
vibrant places full of energy and change. They
absorbed huge numbers of immigrants from rural
Wales and offered them relatively high wages. But by
the 1930s they were ravaged by economic depression
and their people are often crudely represented to us as
either bursting with revolutionary fervour or as cowed
and beaten. In fact, the unique cultural life of the
valleys was formed by and in opposition to the
development of the capitalist mode of production in a
once rural area. What Llewellyn does is to see the early
years of industrial growth as a relatively tranquil
extension of the old rural life. And his account of the
old, pastoral Wales is a rather more sophisticated
version of the kind of nineteenth century writing I
have discussed. The break with the past is not
associated with the introduction and development of a
new mode of production. It is located at the point
where putative rural values yield to industrial forms of
life. At the point, that is, of a growth in collective
power and organised working class resistance. The
rupture with the past is overtly pointed out to us and is
also demonstrated through the break up of the Morgan
family. To describe this, Llewellyn has drawn from
literary sources an almost perfect narrator.

The book is about a boy growing up within a
family, and this familiar device of a child coming to
consciousness of people and events establishes Huw's
innocence and impartiality. These qualities are carried
over into his adult life, so that we are inclined to trust
his judgments and opinions. Moreover, he is not a
visitor, an outsider, but is presented as 'one of us', an
'ordinary worker'. His tone is ingratiatingly populist
and he represents seemingly innocent virtues: he is for
simplicity against complexity; the native over the
foreign; straight talking and action in place of devious
backbiting; craft skills rather than industrial work.

For the first time in his life he is leaving the valley, '. . . to try and find out what is the matter with me and the people I know, because there is something radically wrong with us all, to be sure' (p.68). In fact, there is no reason for him to travel anywhere as his own story of the past offers a coherent enough explanation of what is wrong with the people around him. Central to our understanding of their present sickness is his account of the disintegration of his own family. And what a family it is. Hard-working, prosperous, diligent and creative; one brother invents a coal-cutting machine and a motor car; another plays rugby for Wales. They sing before the Queen at Windsor Palace and they run the Union. They spend their evenings in cultural pursuits and their special domestic occasions, such as weddings, attract hundreds of people, harpists, even entire choirs to their door.

The forms, relationships and structures of family life that Llewellyn asks us to accept and approve of are crucial to the novel. It is, above all, a patriarchal family. The father, Gwilym, is the head of the household and a significant figure in the largely invisible community of which the family is a part. His patriarchal stance is overt and celebrated. When he quarrels with two of his sons they leave home to lodge in the village. Their mother, Beth, brings about a reconciliation, but when they return Gwilym tells them:

> We are all to be lodgers here. . . . No man shall
> say he is father of a house unless his word is
> to be obeyed. Mine is not, so I am not a
> father, but somebody paying for his keep. I am a
> lodger . . . (p.53)

The house is reorganised to accommodate the sons and Huw is moved out of the bedroom he shares with them to a wall bed in the kitchen, where he continues to sleep for many years – a number of them as a bedridden invalid.

This establishes another of Huw's strengths as narrator and central character. In the course of the book he learns what the community expects of him as a man and what characteristics he should display. He learns this not only by direct training from his father and brothers, but also by opposition to the clear roles established for his sisters. Huw becomes an apt pupil in manliness, but his years in the kitchen, at the heart of the world of women, gives him a certain understanding of the hardship of domestic labour. During his long illness he spends a great deal of time listening to women's conversation and is able, more than any other character, to live in both male and female worlds. He frequently sympathises with the hard and limited life of his sister, but this emotion usually only extends to a profound sense of relief that he has been born a boy. But even as a child he argues against the double standard for women when an unmarried, pregnant 'pit girl' is brought before the chapel deacons, while her partner escapes public humiliation. Indeed, Huw stands up in the chapel and publicly argues with the deacons – not the only hint we are given that this boy, who becomes a carpenter, has Christ-like qualities.

The nature of a patriarchal family and of rigidly enforced gender divisions of labour and standards of behaviour is extensively explored by Llewellyn, and its presence in the text needs to be noted, even though he celebrates a sentimentalised and reactionary view of it. None of the main women characters has paid employment, and women who work in the pit are only mentioned as objects of scorn and derision. The Morgan women spend their time in domestic tasks and in the support of their men. Beth is the most stereotypical of the women characters and she embodies many of the virtues of the Welsh mother as that figure is represented in literature. Beth is the organiser and central support of family life. Responsible for the family budgeting, she has a little store of money even in the leanest times. Her lack of formal education – her ignorance – is a minor comic motif which runs through the text; she cannot, for example, follow a map or understand the use of a decimal point. But this also draws attention to her deep wisdom, which is not a matter of book learning but is inherent to her as a woman. The source of this wisdom (in such accounts) is the relationship women have to the past. As Jeanette Marks put it:

> In the Welsh women who sit by the ingle fire of this cottage life one feels an age old continuity of home, of the heart of things, of association, of service, of beauty. . . Much of the colour of that mediaeval world [of the Mabinogion] is a thing of the past, but not its women: they are essentially the same.[9]

Beth and her daughter-in-law Bronwen carry this continuity of tradition. And it is not unimportant that Huw falls in love with Bronwen, who has helped to bring him up and is a woman very like his mother.

But if Bronwen carries traditional values into another generation, Huw's sister Angharad represents the changes that have come to the society. She falls in love with Mr Gruffydd the Nonconformist minister who is a close friend of the family and an important character in the book. He has set out in a desultory sort of way to conduct a great religious revival, but also acts as tutor to Huw and as his moral mentor. Despite the fact that he loves Angharad, he feels that he cannot marry on his small stipend. She eventually contracts a loveless marriage with Iestyn Evans, the son of a coal owner. In so doing she abandons the values of the community in favour of wealth and 'Englishness'. In consequence, she loses her wild, charming and affectionate Welsh ways and becomes cold and hard. This is only one of several misalliances in the book as the old life breaks down against the pressure of new forces.

Not that the old way of life is free of all contradictions. If home is a place of creative development and emotional support, Huw's move to the National School brings him sharply into contact with tension and conflict. He is forbidden to speak Welsh: 'He must on no account be allowed to speak that jargon in or out of school' (p. 163). And he falls out with his bullying and sarcastic teacher Mr Elijah Jonas-Sessions. This man seems to take immediate dislike to Huw both on class grounds ('Your dirty coal mining ways are not wanted here') and because Huw is representative of a kind of Welshness that Jonas-Sessions is anxious to suppress in himself, posturing as he does as a middle class Englishman. Here Llewellyn has the opportunity to explore serious issues in a subtle way, to examine the tensions between an English culture which seemed to offer opportunities for advancement against the traditional, communal values of the world that is structured by Welsh. But this is ignored in favour of a story of individual action. Beaten up by the other boys, Huw is told by his father that he will have to learn to defend himself:

> A boy shall learn to fight, or let him put skirts about his knees. This boy has never been taught to fight, but he shall have his first lesson tonight. We shall see if the National Schools can beat a Morgan. (p. 180)

Huw's boxing lessons are conducted by two specialists, the prize fighter Dai Bando and his friend Cyfartha Lewis. These two are another Welsh 'couple' and very important minor characters. Inarticulate, but humorous, strong and loyal, they speak to each other in terms of endearment, make a strong appeal to male bonding, and embody the values of the community in an unquestioning and naturalised way. On the one night that Huw reluctantly attends a prize fight, Dai Bando is blinded in the ring, but is still able, in the final dramatic scene, to help the Morgans save the pit.

They train Huw to fight and he sets about beating all the boys one by one after school. His success allows him to live quietly enough, and he adopts a stance of passive resistance to Mr Jonas-Sessions and refuses to work at school. He scarcely needs to, as his education is already well in advance of that of the other students. It comes as no surprise to us when he is told that he could win a scholarship to Oxford, for at home he has been reading Euclid, Shakespeare and Dr Johnson for years. Huw is given, from within his community, an education in fist fighting, but also in scholarship and high culture. As he says of his morning boxing lessons, 'So I went from Dai Bando and Cyfartha Lewis, in to Pericles and John Stuart Mill'(p.202). Interestingly, there are no Welsh writers in the family pantheon. Classical learning and a standard English canon are the components of their scholarship. This may appear to be a curious lapse in a book in which Englishness is seen as a pernicious condition. But this Englishness is always undifferentiated and vague. It does not, for example, include major institutions of the British state such as Parliament, and the monarchy is constantly treated with awe and reverence. Nor does the language used in the book help to clarify this position. The most obvious marker of Welshness in the book is the way in which the characters speak. A few examples:

> Come, my pretty one. . . . We will get into the trap and go home, is it?. . . . Come you my little heart and have rest. (p.120)

Two things in the world I do hate. One is talking
behind the back, and the other is lice. So you should
know what I do think of you. (p.60)

'Back me,' I said, 'quick, too.'
'Not yet boy,' Mervyn said, 'I want to hear what
they are going to do.'
'Stay you, then,' I said, 'but I am going from by
here now.' (p.33)

The book is predicated on the notion that the
characters are speaking in Welsh and that what is on
the page is an English translation. This is, after all, a
usual enough device for a novel set in a foreign
country. The problem for Anglo-Welsh texts is that a
real struggle was taking place between the two
languages. A simple 'translation' leaves unexamined
the power relationships inherent in language use. This
is compounded in *How Green Was My Valley* by the
fact that there is little connection between the speech of
its characters and the English spoken by the people of
South Wales, nor is the language of the novel translated
Welsh. It is, in fact, an imaginary speech, created out
of an amalgam of real dialect and literary speech. So
the various discourses in play within the language
remain unnuanced and empty; and the materiality of
language is undermined as its discourses are displaced
from a general structure of language use. The problem
of finding an appropriate language faced all those
British writers who were distanced by class or region
from the centres of cultural power. They adopted a
number of strategies, from the painstaking reproduction of dialect to Lewis Grassic Gibbon's poetically
charged inverted language. Llewellyn's imaginary
speech is very useful for his purpose – the construction
of a romance – as it allows exotic speech to be passed
off as ordinary talk, and he uses it to bind together his

tight, organic community that is under threat from a powerful and alien industrial world.

In the book the central signifier of the corruption of an old, organic way of life is the slag heaps that surround the village and grow over the years to monstrous proportions. Of course, the fact that areas of natural beauty are despoiled by the detritus of extractive industry had often been noted. Joseph Keating observed that on his return to the village of Mountain Ash around 1910:

> . . . the ancient streets were no longer pleasant and picturesque, but grimy with coal dust. Hundreds of new streets, long and straight and ugly, and terrible hills of pit refuse, filled the fields in which I had played. The Cynon river was nothing but flowing mud. . . . All semblance of its former silvery winding was gone.[10]

Keating's response to this industrialisation of the once rural valleys is typical of other observers':

> In many parts the mountains and farms themselves were being buried under pit rubbish. Black industrialism would not stop until it had utterly destroyed the old pastoral life.[11]

Industry, then is both ugly and ravenous; not only does it stain the fields of his childhood, but it possesses an almost demonic energy in its will to destroy 'the old pastoral life'. What is at stake here is a Blakean vision of innocence against experience, as the old, calm pastoral is corrupted by the new, filthy industrial. We are not invited to look at the human experience of the 'old pastoral', which was not nearly as tranquil or idyllic a way of life as this passage might suggest. Instead, Keating asks us to share his response to the sight of the new Mountain Ash, and this response is not one of simple condemnation:

> Yet seeing all the faults of my home did not alter my affection for it. The contrast between the romantic hills and the sordid pit-works in the valley gave me the vision of true sympathy for the lacerated heart of the place.[12]

This contrast between 'sordid pit-works' and 'romantic hills' has been employed by many writers to describe both the valleys themselves and the relationship between the valleys and the rest of Wales.

Keating's response is that of a person coming 'home' after a long absence and seeing the village he has known and remembered, through fresh eyes. This gaze of the returned traveller is one way in which judgments can be made on communities that are 'hidden from view'. Keating's response is to see his old home as *landscape* and to generate from the appearance of the land itself a feeling about what has happened to it: to move from landscape to people and then to an emotional reaction to the 'lacerated heart of the place' when compared with its past. Land, memory, history and culture come together in this way in much writing about Wales. Of course, 'the land' is not simply there; it is complexly coded, containing as it does the same density and contradictions that 'nation' does for other peoples. But if this land is a special place – beloved, longed for, lodged forever in the hearts of its many exiles – it is also (in what is more than a casual metaphor) a body. And, in the case of the valleys, a body whose heart is lacerated. A body that has been raped, corrupted, defiled and scarred; such words are not unusual in descriptions of the industrial South. The corruption and violation of the valleys has to be set against a presumed purity and beauty of the 'real'

Wales. We have already seen how Wales was constructed as innocent, as a place of nature, by nineteenth century writers who visited it. But one tradition of Welsh thought has also seen Wales as a place of purity. In 1900, the Rev. Thomas Jones of Llanelli asserted that 'the Welsh rural areas are still the location of "Hen Wlad y Menyg Gwynion" (the old land of pure morals); only the southern industrial valleys have been corrupted through the influence of English people and their vicious habits.'[13]

Llewellyn, too, sees the English as carriers of the bacillus of industrialism and as helping to destroy the old, pure Welsh way of life. The slag heaps are the first thing Huw notices when he is carried from his invalid's bed up the mountain. But the tip is not simply out there as part of the landscape; it grows, by the end of the book, so as to press on the house itself, and will soon destroy what we now have to see as both the Morgans' house and the House of Morgan. All that saves it is the soundness and virtues of the past:

> Here, in this quiet house I sit thinking back to the structure of my life, building again that which has fallen. . . .
>   The slag heap is moving again. I can hear it whispering to itself, and as it whispers, the walls of this brave little house are girding themselves to withstand the assault. For months, more than I ever thought it would have the courage to withstand, that great mound has borne down upon these walls, this roof. And for those months the great bully has been beaten, for in my father's day men built well for they were craftsmen. Stout beams, honest blocks, good work, and love for the job, all that is in this house. (pp.96–7)

Craft skills are important in the book, and are

associated with the old ways of working. Huw leaves the colliery and becomes a master carpenter. But, if he stays much longer in this house, not even the strength of the past will save him; he will be crushed to death as, at the end of the book, his father is crushed 'like a beetle' underground while trying to save the pit from the revolutionary fervour of the mob.

Also pressing against the old way of life is the presence of 'foreigners' who are described as 'half breed Welsh, Irish and English . . . the dross of the collieries'. These people live in a few streets of the town and the only character to be drawn from their number (making a very brief appearance) is Idris Atkinson. The 'swine' who murders a child is discovered and handed over by Mr Gruffydd (as God's representative) to the men who tracked him down for summary vengeance and execution. One point of this extremely unpleasant chapter is to assure us that the community is capable of taking care of its own system of justice. This lays claim to be 'Welsh' law and is seen as antithetical to a bureaucratic English system of police, courts, magistrates and all the formal apparatus of juridical authority. The basis of authority for the *How Green Was My Valley* version of Welsh law is conformity to vaguely invoked laws of God and to the traditional mores of community. This law is often indistinguishable from patriarchal authority and is enforced by male retribution. When Mr Elias steals the Morgans' turkeys Gwilym seizes them back from him, having rejected his son Davy's suggestion that he go to the police: 'Why should we invite the police? I will be my own police while I have health and strength'(p.135). Mr Elias is not strong enough to resist Gwilym: '"I will have the English Law on you," said Old Elias, in a woman's high voice, with tears in his eyes.' Gwilym tosses him into an apple barrel, threatens to burn his shop about him if he does not leave the valley, and tells him he has 'had a bit of Welsh law tonight' (p.141). This incident makes clear the conflation between 'I will be my own police' and 'Welsh law' and the connections of both with male strength, against Old Elias's 'womanly' appeal to English systems of justice.

Welsh patriarchal law is invoked in serious matters of murder and theft, but its more frequent use throughout the novel is in the regulation of sexual relationships. For example, Huw faces the 'English' courts when he beats up a man who has made innuendoes about his relationship with Bronwen. The case is dismissed because the man he has attacked recognises that he has received his just deserts. Earlier, Huw had been out on the mountain at night with a young woman whose absence from home is noticed; men with torches search for them and when Huw manages to get home without being discovered, his brother asks him, '"Do you want the men of the other Valley round here to burn the village?. . . Every man here is waiting for it to start," Owen said. "Not a man is in bed"' (p.312). These repeated threats of correction by fire are more than simple homage to the Welsh love of a good blaze. It both connects us with biblical ideas of elemental punishment and also hints at rural patterns of revolt such as rick-burning. However, the control of women is usually achieved more simply. When Iestyn Evans speaks to Angharad in the street, her brother knocks him down; 'London tricks' is Ianto's opinion of this unauthorised greeting. However he warns Angharad:

> I will not allow my sister to be treated like a pit-
> woman. . . . Next time, if there is a next time, I will
> kill him. If he wants to speak to you, let him ask
> permission. We have a home and he knows where it
> is. (p.155)

Iestyn is the son of old Mr Evans, the owner/manager of a small coal mine and friend of the Morgans. He approves of Ianto's action as he is himself an adherent of the values of the community in which he lives. We are told that he pays his workers well and is concerned for their welfare, unlike other coal-owners. Mr Evans is killed in the pit, like many of his men, and we are given the impression that his life does not differ in major respects from that of the rest of the people in the village. This implicit similarity between the lives of coal-owner and workers points up the absence of any exploration of complex class relation-ships in the book. Such an absence is not confined to *How Green Was My Valley*; it is true of much of the fiction about industrial South Wales. One obvious but important reason for this is that these overwhelmingly working class communities lacked a developed bourgeoisie, so that there was little immediate class antagonism. They were close-knit communities linked together by shared values, class position and work within a single industry.

Another, perhaps more important reason is a belief that 'Welshness' excludes class. In *The Dragon Has Two Tongues*, Glyn Jones says of Wales:

Class as understood in England is largely trans-cended here by the fact of common speech, a common religious faith and common political aspirations. To these factors it owed its social homogeneity.[14]

But he adds that class

certainly existed in the valleys and class struggles took place. But these often devastating encounters were, in a sense, impersonal. People inevitably suffered in them . . . but they suffered, it seems to me, less individually and in isolation than as part of the whole community to which they belonged.

This idea that Welshness transcends class has, of course, frequently been challenged. While there is no space here to rehearse the arguments that Wales is not the cosily homogeneous society Jones would have us believe, it is worth noting that his definition of class is a matter of common habits and styles of living rather than a relationship to the means of production. Community and communality are for Jones, and many other Welsh writers, set against class rather than being derived from it. In *How Green Was My Valley*, as we have seen, a particular kind of community is held up to us for praise. It is a place in which the putative homogeneity of Welsh society is threatened by the importation of new ideas and ways of acting. Not the least important of these is the growth of a unionisation that goes beyond the immediacy of local struggle: for Llewellyn what finally destroys the community is class action which he sees as the action of 'cattle' and sets against the nobility of an individual fight.

A kind of workers' struggle dominates the book, but this is not seen as arising out of any determinate mode of production, or even as workers in opposition to owners and managers. 'Your enemy is usury,' Mr Graffydd tells the miners (p.144), and this together with 'lazy lordlings and greedy shareholders' and 'middle men' constructs the class enemy as remote landowners and finance capitalists. Ianto, back from a spell of work in London, tells a group of men: 'That is where your proper wages are spent. If you are content to see what should be going into your pocket, falling into the pockets of landlords, and bankers and Jews, and on the backs of whores, I am not'(p.200). 'Landlords, bankers and Jews' were of course perceived as the enemy in the 1930s, by many people who subscribed to a petit-bourgeois analysis of the contemporary crisis. There can be no doubt that many found Llewellyn's construction of Wales very attractive.

We should remember that he was not free to invent any version of Wales, simply from the resources of his imagination. He had to make connections with ideas and conceptions readers already cherished, even though these were for the most part in circulation not as ideas, but as 'natural' ways of feeling and responding. The power of the text derives from the way in which it uses romance to take real historical struggles and return them to us as an ineluctable fall from grace of particular human beings. 'Welshness' becomes a cover under which highly specific analyses and ideological stances are smuggled into the book as unproblematic and natural. In other words, Llewellyn creates a 'common sense' world which claims to derive its authenticity from its direct address to Welsh experience. But what is presented as particular and local is in fact part of a much more general and dominant ideology.

The Morgan family is irrevocably broken by exile and death. Only Huw remains, and he will soon leave the valley. The novel is cyclical and ends as it begins; it offers us no way out. Its nostalgia, too, can only return us, longing but helpless, to another time. The past cannot affect or change the present; it is sealed away and our only access to it is through the individual act of memory. This is Llewellyn's essential position and we can see why, at the outbreak of war in 1939, it carried great emotional appeal. It is significant, though, that from its first edition the book has never been out of print; the social constructions and accounts of the past which it helps to keep in circulation need to be understood and challenged if we are to find radical solutions to the recurrent crises of Wales.

Notes

1 See, for example, Glyn Tegai Hughes, 'The mythology of the mining valleys', *Triskel 2*, Llandybie, Christopher Davies, 1973, and especially, Dai Smith, *Wales! Wales?*, London, Allen & Unwin, 1984.

2 See Raymond Williams, 'The Welsh industrial novel', in *Problems in Materialism and Culture*, London, Verso, 1980.

3 Richard Llewellyn, *How Green Was My Valley*, London, Michael Joseph, 1939. This and subsequent quotations are from the 26th impression of the 1st edition, 1942.

4 Anne Beale, *The Vale of the Towey: Or Sketches in South Wales*, London, Longman, 1844, p.vii.

5 Ibid.

6 Frances Burnett, *Miss Crespigny*, London, Routledge, 1878, p.11.

7 Bertha Thomas, *Picture Tales from Welsh Hills*, London, T. Fisher Unwin, 1912, p.34.

8 See Sally Jones, *Allen Raine*, Cardiff, University of Wales Press, 1979.

9 Jeanette Marks, *Gallant Little Wales*, London, Constable, 1912, p.143.

10 Joseph Keating, *My Struggle for Life*, London, Simpkin Marshall & Co., 1916, p.269.

11 Ibid.

12 Ibid., p.270.

13 Quoted in Russell Davies, 'In a broken dream', *Llafur*, vol.3, no.4, 1983, p.24.

14 Glyn Jones, *The Dragon Has Two Tongues*, London, Dent, 1968, pp.14–15.

Marguerite Radclyffe Hall, by Charles Buchell, 1918 (National Portrait Gallery)

5

An inverted romance: The Well of Loneliness *and sexual ideology*

JEAN RADFORD

Of the crop of novels about homosexual love produced after the First World War – Rosamund Lehmann's *Dusty Answer*, MacKenzie's *Extraordinary Women*, Bowen's *The Hotel*, Woolf's *Orlando* and Radclyffe Hall's *The Well of Loneliness* – it was Hall's novel which became and has remained by far the most popular. For whether one defines the popular as non-canonical, or oppositional, or simply as that kind of writing which attempts to popularise more specialised forms of discourse, *The Well of Loneliness* can claim to fulfil all these conditions. The reasons for its popularity are themselves worth considering.

First, the novel was *designed* and written to reach a wide audience, as 'John' Radclyffe Hall herself made clear and as her biographer-lover Una, Lady Troubridge confirms: 'she had long wanted to write a book on sexual inversion, a novel that would be accessible to the general public who did not have access to technical treatises.'[1] The use of Havelock Ellis's sexual theories and the borrowings from heterosexual romance forms are both in service of Hall's passionate demand that the homosexual's 'right to existence' be recognised. Her theoretical and literary tools – the very shape of the narrative – were geared to this self-conscious project of winning the consent of 'normal' heterosexual society.

The second, most potent, reason for its popularity

97

concerns the circumstances of its production. The Obscenity trial which followed its appearance in 1928 gave *The Well* a notoriety which in one sense is still active: almost all the subsequent editions refer back to that moment – the moment when Douglas, editor of the *Sunday Express*, said he'd 'rather give a healthy boy or girl a phial of prussic acid than this novel'. Under such conditions, as Claudia Stillman Franks says in *Beyond the Well of Loneliness*, 'The Well could not fail to be a best seller.'[2] The attempt to suppress it not only launched it as an underground classic but also mobilised large numbers of writers, intellectuals and liberals on its behalf. The list of those offering to speak for it, in both the English and American trials, confirms this effect. So, if the author's own project was to break 'the tyranny of silence' surrounding homosexual love, it was the state's intervention (via the Director of Public Prosecutions) which amplified that voice and gave the novel its home among the liberalising discourses of the 1920s.

But, third, its readership since 1928 to the present depends on the fact that the protest-plea for homosexuality is still one that needs to be made. (In the introduction to the recent Virago edition (1982), Alison Hennegan vividly describes the ways in which *The Well* is still used in lesbian subcultures.) Although the ideological, social and political conditions governing sexuality *have* changed, there is enough cultural continuity between the England of 1928 and the England of fifty or more years later to give this narrative of lesbianism a continuing relevance. The readings now made are different, but it is read as a story for lesbians as well as a story for those who wish to understand more about women's sexuality.

This brings me to the fourth and, in my view, most important reason for its continuing popularity: that the very mixed and contradictory discourses on sexuality in play in this novel (medical, psychoanalytic and religious) are still in play and still unresolved in today's discussions. If *The Well* remains – as Jane Rule claims – '*the* lesbian novel',[3] this is partly because no 'metalanguage' about homosexuality (or sexuality) has been produced since. When we read *The Well of Loneliness* now, we do so not simply to examine a set of archaic and superseded discourses about sexuality, but *from within* a set of equally problematic debates on the social, psychic or biological determinants of sexuality and object-choice. For though much has been written in the last fifteen years, particularly from the American and European women's movements, on the question of women's sexuality, little has been resolved, I would argue. And though feminist critics have challenged *The Well*'s religiosity, its defeatism, its endorsement (in some sense) of a conventional patriarchal notion of sexual difference, its rejection of a lesbian subculture in favour of role-playing coupledom,[4] it remains nevertheless a doubly significant text: for what it tells us about sexual ideologies in the 1920s, and for the way it speaks to contemporary sexual ideologies. The fascination of *The Well*, for me, read in this way, is that it alerts us to the discontinuities and the continuities in the way we tell stories about human sexuality. It can tell us more about what we can no longer say and what we continue to try to say because – as Foucault puts it – we are within the same archive.[5]

For the last few years I've been using *The Well of Loneliness* in teaching a course entitled 'The crisis in consciousness 1890–1930' at Hatfield Polytechnic. I find it immensely useful as a discussion point in introducing Freud's theory of sexuality and contrasting this with that of the English sexologist Havelock Ellis, from whom Hall took her definition of the 'invert'.

Havelock Ellis's *Studies in the Psychology of Sex* which appeared from 1896 to 1910 were enormously influential at that time and Hall considered herself a 'humble but very gladly willing disciple' of his.

The main points I try to bring out in this context are basically those made by Jeffrey Weeks and Juliet Mitchell:[6] that Ellis's theory of inverts was biologically determinist, that he tends to see sexuality as an essence – a biological instinct whose direction (the object-choice) is governed by the number of chromosomes in the individual. Freud, in contrast, argued for a more mobile concept of the sexual drive; that instead of being essentially hetero or homosexual drive, human sexuality only arrives at heterosexual genital expression through a number of diverse routes and channels themselves socially constructed within the family. Far from being innate or 'natural' (and thus 'discovered', as Stephen Gordon does with hers in *The Well*), sexuality is considered as a polymorphous and unstable force which is only eventually and precariously established in its adult heterosexual form. The difficulty with Freud's theory, as Ellis was quick to note, was that it implied that this 'most fundamental' of human instincts could equally well be adapted to 'sterility' as to the propagation of the race. 'Such a theory is unworkable,' he claimed in 'Sexual inversion',[7] and maintained a distinction between hereditary and cultural forms of homosexuality: true 'inversion' was congenital, caused by hereditary factors, whereas cultural forms of homosexuality were 'perversions'.

Without going further into these contrasting theories of sexuality here – Jeffrey Weeks discusses Ellis's work in some detail in *Socialism and the New Life* – both the determinist (Ellis) and the psychoanalytic (Freudian) conceptions of sexuality are at work in the text. These ideological contradictions in the presentation of the heroine's sexual development are particularly striking,

visible even to readers not familiar with the sexual
debates of the period. I would like to argue that this
'over-determination' of Stephen Gordon's homosexuality creates a tension, an ambivalence which is
central to its meaning for Hall's contemporaries and for
readers today.

In the opening chapters, for example, the mother's
inability to love the heroine Stephen Gordon is
explained at one level by the fact she has an 'unnatural'
daughter. Coming, we are told, 'from a race of
devoted mothers', Anna Gordon's estrangement from
her own child is a source of distress and mystery. Only
when Stephen is exposed by a neighbour as an 'invert'
(who had made love to his wife) is this maternal
rejection *explained* (away). The mother's story of their
relationship at this point poses Stephen's inversion as
cause and her failure of maternal love as *effect*:

> 'All your life I've felt very strangely towads you' she
> was saying, 'I've felt a kind of physical repulsion, a
> desire not to touch or to be touched by you – a
> terrible thing for a mother to feel – it has often made
> me deeply unhappy. I've often felt that I was being
> unjust, unnatural – but now I know that my instinct
> was right; it is you who are unnatural, not
> I. . . .'(200)[8]

Anna's self-justification depends on the 'congenital'
explanation which is upheld in the rest of the narrative,
but it is also possible to read these chapters in a
different way: that Stephen Gordon is unable to take
up a feminine position because of her mother's
'repulsion' and lack of love. Stephen's father, Sir
Philip, is used to voice this different construction in the
scene between the two parents where he denounces his
wife's role:

'Cruelty, yes, but not Stephen's, Anna – it's yours;
for in all the child's life you've never loved her.'(111)

Though the authorial voice calls this 'a terrible half-truth', the point is made: that the mother's hostility may be the *cause* not the *consequence* of Stephen's inversion. Sexual inversion can be explained through family dynamics as well as chromosones.

Unable to take up a rival feminine position because of her hostile mother, she identifies with the loving parent and his masculinity. She defends herself against her mother's rejection by a 'reaction-formation', converts the painful anger into idealisation, and the feminine is taken as the love-object. In Lacanian terms, she takes the loved one's (i.e. her father's) desire as her own:

'But for his sake she must love the thing that he
loved, her mother . . .'(86)

Interestingly enough, these sections evoked most discussion with the students I worked with. For in addition to being the story of an artist's development (a *Kunstlerroman*) and the story of an invert's development (*Bildungsroman*), *The Well* is the story of a woman's complex negotiation of sexual difference within the family. And many women readers, heterosexual as well as lesbian, can identify with the difficulties of adopting the feminine role within a patriarchal family culture.[9]

The novel supports both these readings and in addition offers a third, more social level of determination with details of the parents' desire for a son, their giving her a male name, the 'masculine' role expectations and education she receives. Not least of these social factors is the sharply polarised nature of the gender roles described in this late Victorian/Edwardian upper class milieu. The neighbouring children, Roger and Violet Antrim, epitomise the gender divisions: the freedom and activity possible for the boy and the limitations imposed on the feminine Violet. Stephen's envious resentment of Roger's maleness (he is later to become her rival in love) may be seen as part of her inverted nature, or as penis envy, but it can also be read at the social level as a powerful comment on male privilege in a patriarchal world:

> . . . envied his right to climb trees and play cricket and football – his right to be perfectly natural; above all she envied his splendid conviction that being a boy constituted a privilege in life; she could well understand that conviction, but this only increased her envy. (47)

The narrative of *The Well* signals its dependence on these conflicting theories of homosexuality not just implicitly but through a scattering of explicit references to medical authorities. Thus on the 'congenital' side, there is the sought-for preface by Havelock Ellis himself; the reference to Ulrichs in chapter 4, whose pamphlets in the 1860s and 1870s defended homosexuality as a hereditary condition and therefore not subject to penalties; then there is the reference to Krafft-Ebing whose marked copy of *Psychopathia Sexualis* (1886) Stephen 'discovers' in her father's library, just after her mother discovers – again through documents – Stephen's homosexual love for Angela Crossby. In addition to these there are repeated references to Stephen's masculine physique in terms which echo those used by Ellis. She is 'a narrow-hipped, wide-shouldered little tadpole of a baby' as soon as she enters the world – thus establishing her as one of Nature or God's true inverts.

Nevertheless, as the story unfolds, a number of

psychoanalytic terms begin to emerge in the text: references to Stephen's sense of her 'incomplete' and 'maimed' body can be linked to the invert's lack of the phallus that should be hers, but they are also linked, via her governess, Puddle, to notions of repression; another character has a 'litter of hefty complexes' (271); Brockett recommends the Hungarian psychoanalyst Ferenczi's paper on 'Introjection and transference' (298) published in 1909; later the word 'libido' is used in a distinctively Freudian sense. But the most striking allusion to psychoanalytic theories occurs in the final scenes of the novel, where Stephen relinquishes her lover Mary to a third person:

> Only one gift could she offer to love, to Mary, and that was the gift of Martin.
>   In a kind of dream she perceived these things. In a dream she now moved and had her being; scarcely conscious of whither this dream would lead, the while her every perception was quickened. And this dream of hers was *immensely compelling*, so that all she did seemed *clearly predestined*; and she *could not have acted otherwise*, nor could she have made a false step, although dreaming.(430) (my italics)

The emphasis on the word 'dream', repeated five times here, suggests an acknowledgment not so much to Freud's theories of dreams but to the psychoanalytic concept of the 'repetition compulsion'. What this dream like state recalls to the reader is that this triangular relationship, and Stephen's behavior within it, has indeed happened before. It is the last in a series of triangles in which the Oedipal renunciation (of the father as love-object) is re-enacted. The heroine may be 'scarcely conscious' of what compels and predestines her decision to give up her lover, but the pattern has been firmly established within the text. From the first

triangle of Stephen-mother-father, to the primal scene
between Stephen-Collins-footman, then to the triangles
with Stephen-Angela-husband and Stephen-Angela-
Roger ('a grotesque triangle' (184)), to the final version
with Stephen-Mary-Martin, ('that curious trinity'
(424)), there is a symmetry to which the authorial voice
continually draws attention. Thus despite (or because
of) the text's silence about Stephen's first seven years,
it's possible to read her subsequent development, and
the plea to God for unconditional love, back to those
unnarrated events of early childhood. In Freudian
terms, Stephen repeats a renunciation – one originally
forced on her by her relationship with her mother –
but also reverses it. Her love for Mary has enabled her
to become the 'good' mother who allows her 'girl' a
male love-object, hence 'the gift of Martin'.[10]

So, despite the seal of approval by Havelock Ellis,
Radclyffe Hall's dependence on 'inversion' theory
seems to me rather like Defoe's use of Providence and
Puritan theology in *Robinson Crusoe*: it acts as an
ideological frame or scaffold, and it has a reserve of
power as does the story of the Prodigal Son in Defoe's
novel, but much of the narrative discourse exceeds and
escapes that frame. Foucault, in *The History of Sexuality*,
describes how scientific and medical discourses about
homosexuality and sexual deviance of the late nineteenth
century:

> made possible the formation of a 'reverse' discourse:
> homosexuality began to speak in its own behalf, to
> demand that its legitimacy or 'naturality' be ack-
> nowledged, often in the same vocabulary. . . .

And he adds:

> There is not, on the one side, a discourse of power,
> and opposite to it, another discourse that runs

counter to it. Discourses are tactical elements or blocks operating in the field of force relations; there can exist different and even contradictory discourses within the same strategy.[11]

The co-existence of contradictory discourses about homosexuality in *The Well* can thus be seen in Foucault's terms, as a 'reverse' discourse, where the object of the medical category 'homosexual' adopts terms like 'inversion' transformatively in order 'to demand legitimacy'. The congenital argument supports the notion that homosexuals are created by Nature, the psychoanalytic elements that they are produced by the family; the important effect of both is to establish that Stephen is not homosexual *by choice* – that she is, as one critic put it, 'absolutely absolved' from all blame or responsibility.[12]

Hall's strategy was to demand recognition for the legitimacy or naturality of homosexuality and her 'tactical blocks' included the major biological, psychological and social discourses in circulation. It was with these blocks that she set out to challenge the oldest and most powerful discourse on homosexuality then still in place: the religious view of it as 'sin and abomination'. For significantly, it is in these, religious, terms that Stephen's mother couches her repudiation and it is to her father's Bible that she turns back after finding the annotated copy of Krafft-Ebing.

As a devout Catholic, Radclyffe Hall was particularly concerned to protest against the Church's attitude to homosexuality, the fact that their 'blessings were strictly reserved for the normal'(405). She thus tranforms Ellis's theory that inversion is part of Nature's scheme to the propostion that inverts are part of God's creation and by means of symbolism constructs a complex religious parable. By giving her heroine the name of the first Christian martyr, by

having her cast out of Eden (Morton), by linking
Stephen's war wound with 'the mark of Cain' – even
her experience of Parisian nightlife is imaged as a
Dantean journey through Hell with Brockett as her
Virgil – Hall leads us inexorably to the final scene: the
closure device where, like Christ, Stephen is crucified
for her kind. In the last two pages of her novel, the
intensification of the prose and the density of biblical
allusions are perhaps the most alienating sections of the
text for the contemporary non-religious reader. (And
not only for the reader now, as Virginia Woolf's
private comments indicate.) To further empower her
plea for tolerance, the writer has her heroine make the
ultimate emotional sacrifice: the renunciation of the
Beloved, Mary. Though her inverted love is God-
given, she is not, it seems, allowed to enjoy it.

The religious parable here converges with the social
protest. For the plea, ostensibly made to God,

> 'God', she gasped, 'we believe; we have told You we
> believe. . . . We have not denied You, then rise up
> and defend us. Acknowledge us, oh God, before the
> whole world. Give us also the right to our existence!'
> (437)

is in effect also addressed to the reader, that is, to *social*
not metaphysical beings. It is finally to *writing*, not
prayer, that Hall the Catholic entrusts the burden of her
belief. The invert's sufferings have been taken out of
the confessional into literature. So, in struggling to free
homosexuality from the religious discourses of 'sin',
from nineteenth century medical discourses of it as
'disease', Radclyffe Hall instigates a new discourse of
the homosexual as a socially oppressed 'victim': an image
which was to become all too popular in twentieth
century writing. She thus performs what the ghost-like
Adolphe Blanc tells Stephen Gordon she must do:

> They are good, these doctors (some of them very
> good; they work hard trying to solve our problems)
> but half the time they must work in the dark – the
> whole truth is known only to the normal invert. The
> doctors cannot make the ignorant think, cannot hope
> to bring home the suffering of millions; only one of
> ourselves can some day do that. (390)

Hall's personal needs, both religious and psychological,
are obviusly very important in this construction of the
homosexual as sacrificial lamb, but there is, I think,
another influence at work.

Just as she adapted a variety of available theories to
present a sympathetic portrait of the lesbian heroine, so
the form of her novel draws on a number of fictional
forms. *The Well*, as I have argued, has elements of
religious parable, case history and social protest novel;
but for the love story and the sacrificial fantasy of the
ending, Hall adapted the forms of heterosexual
romance fiction. In the popular romance, the heroine
also struggles for the right to love against all
impediments, whether these be social convention,
parental pressure or betrayal. In these narratives of
obstructed love, the usual closure to the plot was of
course the union of the lovers, but the renunciation of
human love in favour of the divine was an important
variation. Further, in the romances of Ouida, Marie
Corelli and Florence Barclay, notions of love and
sacrifice are consistently presented in quasi-religious
language very similar to that of *The Well of Loneliness*.
Apart from plot conventions, it is the *style* of *The Well*
which links it most strongly to popular romance
writing of the late nineteenth and early twentieth
century period: the linguistic archaisms, syntactical
inversions, adjectival insistence and exclamatory style.

Hall also follows the conventions of romantic fiction
in this period by setting her heroine in an aristocratic

milieu: her titled parents live on a country estate complete with swans on the lake, hunters in the stables, and the right number of housemaids. What is more, it is an aristocracy enlightened by the intellectual and artistic movements of the day; Anna Gordon and her daughter are painted by Millais, Sir Philip keeps up his classics as well as his riding. This aspect of the story was *not* autobiographical as Hall's biographer, Una Lady Troubridge, points out: 'in *The Well* many of Stephen Gordon's feelings and reactions, though practically none of her circumstances or experiences, were her own'.[13] In the text the 'nobility' of Stephen's origins works as a metaphor for her high moral qualities, but also underlines the extent of her loss when cast out from her rightful inheritance and social position within this organic, near-feudal world. Her heroism in the war, the chivalrous behaviour towards her lovers and the sense of *noblesse oblige* generally maintained, are all of course part of Hall's argument against the invert's assumed degeneracy, but they also correspond to the class fantasies familiar to readers of romance. Stephen Gordon has all the trappings of the romantic hero – with the difference that she is a woman. She has, for example, the same strong sexual passions restrained only by an equally strong sense of honour.

> Honour, good God! Was this her honour? Mary, whose nerves had been strained to breaking! A dastardly thing it would be to drag her through the maze of passion, with no word of warning. (300)

In plot, characterisation and language, then, we can see forms of popular romance writing alongside the realist elements of the social protest fiction. Here, as in so many novels, romance and realism are not oppositional modes but are inextricably intertwined.

It is, it seems to me, a complex irony, that what is now hailed as one of the first 'coming out' novels should depend so heavily on the forms of popular heterosexual romance. For, in medieval romance, it is the hero who is given the love of a woman as his reward, whereas in women's romance, it is the woman who is given the love of the hero. (Her status as heroine is in fact defined on that basis.) But in Radclyffe Hall's inverted romance, the heroine becomes a 'hero' by renouncing the love of a woman: the invert renounces an individual love relationship in the name of the 'suffering millions' of women *and men* for whom the novel speaks, thus revealing another paradoxical use to which romance forms can be put.

Notes

1 Troubridge, Una Lady (1961), *The Life and Death of Radclyffe Hall*, London, Hammond, p.81.

2 Franks, Claudia Stillman (1982), *Beyond the Well of Loneliness*, Amersham, Bucks, Avebury, p.35.

3 Rule, Jane (1976), *Lesbian Images*, London, Peter Davies.

4 See, for example, Stimpson, Catherine, 'Zero degree deviancy', *Critical Enquiry*, vol.8, no.2 (Winter 1981).

5 Foucault, Michel (1972), *The Archeology of Knowledge*, London, Tavistock, p.130.

6 Rowbotham, S. and Weeks, J. (1977) *Socialism and the New Life*, London, Pluto Press.

7 Ellis, Havelock (1936), 'Sexual inversion', in *Studies in the Psychology of Sex*, New York, Random House. Cited in Rowbotham and Weeks, op.cit.,p.164.

8 This and all subsequent page numbers refer to the Permabook edition, New York, 1951.

9 See Chodorow, Nancy (1974), 'Family structure and feminine personality' in *Women, Culture and Society*, ed. Rosaldo, M.Z. and Lamphere, L., Stanford, Calif., Stanford University Press.

10 Post-Freudian psychoanalytic theories might produce a different, less Oedipal reading of Stephen's psychosexual development.

Janine Chasseguet-Smirgel's *Female Sexuality: New Psychological Views* (London, Virago, 1981), for example, opens up a quite different construction of the same material.

11 Foucault, Michel (1981), *The History of Sexuality*, Harmondsworth, Penguin, pp.101–2. For a fuller discussion of 'reverse discourse' see Ruehl, Sonia (1982), 'Inverts and experts: Radclyffe Hall and lesbian identity', in *Feminism, Culture and Politics*, ed. Brunt, R. and Rowan, C., London, Lawrence & Wishart.

12 For a similar statement of the homosexual's lack of choice, see the comment of Nathalie Clifford Baney (the model, supposedly, for Valerie Seymour in *The Well*): 'albinoes aren't reproached for having pink eyes and whitish hair, why should they hold it against me for being a lesbian? It's a question of nature; my queerness isn't a vice, isn't "deliberate", and harms no-one.' Cited in Chalon, J.(1976), translated by Carol Barko(1979), *Portrait of a Seductress*, New York, Crown Publishers, p.47.

13 Troubridge, op.cit.

Vivian Leigh as Scarlett O'Hara in MGM's *Gone With the Wind* (1939)

6
Gone With the Wind:
the mammy of them all

HELEN TAYLOR

Gone With the Wind is one of the best selling books of all time, an astonishing publishing phenomenon. An instant success when it appeared in 1936, it has sold over 16 million hardback copies, and still sells over 100,000 hard copies each year (as well as many more paperbacks). Translated into twenty-seven languages, it has been published successfully in thirty-seven countries. The David Selznick film – like the book showered with awards, when it came out in 1939 – continues to be screened all over the world, and is regarded as one of the most popular films ever made.

As soon as I mentioned *Gone With the Wind* to women friends, all enthusiastically described their readings (though I have met few men who have read it); several of these women knew it back to front, having allowed themselves the 'three bathroom readings' to which Rachel Brownstein admits.[1] Many had seen the film countless times. Since I started looking, *Gone With the Wind* has seemed to be everywhere. One week in May 1984, MGM celebrated its sixtieth anniversary by giving a London screening to the film, 'the daddy of them all' as movie magazines call it; and a 'Scarlett' advertised for her 'Rhett' in the *New Statesman* personal column. Meanwhile a local Bristol pub held a 'Gone With the Wind Night' featuring 'Deep South fancy dress', bourbon and

113

beans. Every epic popular novel written by women, from the Australian Colleen McCullough and Scots Reay Tannahill to the Chinese Han Suyin, seems to be advertised and given a blurb by comparison with the Margaret Mitchell original. One of the most familiar Left posters of recent years is the Socialist Workers Party montage of Mrs Thatcher/Scarlett O'Hara being borne to bed by Ronald Reagan/Rhett Butler while the nuclear bomb/American Civil War explodes in the distance.[2]

It is interesting that in recent years the text (book and film) has tended to attract uncritical enthusiasm or good-natured amusement; although at the time it appeared, its idealisation of the Old South and racist revival of neo-Confederate sympathies for antebellum social and racial relations came under considerable attack, these are today widely regarded as matters for the historian or pedant. While white feminists flock to see the movie, and the novel features in a hagiographical study of southern women's writing,[3] it is left to Black women to point to the political problems raised by book and film. Toni Morrison and Alice Walker have both used Scarlett O'Hara as a symbol of the white womanhood which has belittled them and led to lynchings of their men. Toni Morrison's character Guitar expresses anger at the stomping to death in Mississippi of a Black boy who 'whistled at some Scarlett O'Hara cunt'[4]; Walker's narrator writes to 'Lucy' to tell her why, though both are feminists, she snubbed her at the 'Women for Elected Officials Ball'. The requirement was that women dress up as the feminist they most admire; Lucy had come as Scarlett. The angry narrator, telling Lucy of the difficulties Black women have in refusing negative stereotypes and images of themselves, recalls a different *Gone With the Wind* from that cherished by white women:[5]

My trouble with Scarlett was always the forced
buffoonery of Prissy [the young Black slave who
claims falsely to be able to deliver babies] whose
strained, slavish voice, as Miz Scarlett pushed her so
masterfully up the stairs, I could never get out of my
head.

As Alice Walker well demonstrates, there are various
problems posed by the popular success of *Gone With
the Wind*, most notably the relationship of women
readers to its feminist sub-text and central female
protagonist. Scarlett O'Hara's mingled determination,
competence, and vulnerability are qualities with which
women readers identify, and which make the book/film
popular reference points. But I would argue that for a
reader to celebrate the text's feminism must involve
both turning a blind eye to its white supremacist
southern propaganda, and entering into an unholy
alliance with the crudest southern chauvinism and the
activities of the Ku Klux Klan, an organisation once
again experiencing a strong revival in the Deep South.

With popular literature of many kinds, this dilemma
exists for feminist readers; too often we find ourselves
uncomfortably but deliciously identifying with the
'wrong' kinds of women in terms of feminist/socialist
ideology and practice. Aristocratic and bourgeois
models of feminity which we may refuse in our own
lives are nevertheless profoundly attractive to our
fantasies, and powerful in our emotional memories. In
political terms, especially dangerous is the romance set
in a historical period and place which are unknown,
thus 'exotic' to us as readers. For most British women,
Mitchell's partisan version of the Civil War and
Reconstruction in Georgia will be read unreflectively;
the political argument and context of the novel will
either be absorbed uncritically, or – I suspect – ignored
through selective skipping. As with the exotic contexts

of Mills & Boon romantic novels – a plantation in Brazil, a tax haven in Monte Carlo, a privately owned Greek island – the socio-political 'setting' is read as just that: a site on which social relations are reduced to interpersonal relations which are constructed as natural, eternal, and uncontradictory – in keeping with the function of feminine romance as 'the bourgeois mode of pastoral'.[6]

A compressed plot summary will remind readers of the story, and help make sense of the article to the uninitiated. The novel takes place during the Civil War and Reconstruction (the period of Northern Federal rule in the South). It opens just as the Civil War begins; Scarlett O'Hara of the large slave-holding Tara Plantation, Clayton County, Georgia, loves Ashley Wilkes who marries the angelic Melanie. Scarlett's almost unrequited love for the tortured Ashley both prevents her happiness with three husbands and provides much of the emotional tension throughout the book. Captain Rhett Butler, an apparent scallawag (Yankee collaborator who is really firmly on the Confederate side) meets and admires Scarlett. After she has gone to stay in Atlanta, Rhett helps her and Melanie to escape from the city which is being burned down by Sherman's marching troops. Scarlett, who had married to get revenge on Ashley Wilkes, is widowed in the war and consorts with Rhett to the scandal of her Atlanta relatives and friends. She returns to the pillaged Tara to find her mother dead and father virtually insane. Ruthlessly stealing Frank, her sister's beau, she marries him to get money to pay Federal taxes on the plantation; he is later killed while participating in a Ku Klux Klan raid. She agrees to marry Rhett Butler, who builds her a grand house on Peachtree Street, Atlanta. But they are unhappy; love of Ashley and fear of pregnancy (as with her earlier marriages) make her sexually cold. Their beloved daughter Bonnie dies jumping her horse. Rhett leaves, and too late Scarlett realises how much she loves him. She resolves to return to Tara to lick her wounds and decide how to get him back.

Margaret Mitchell (1900–1949) wrote her own autobiography obliquely in *Gone With the Wind*. While a journalist, she had experimented with short plays, an autobiographical novel and short stories, and a conventional 'tragic mulatto' miscegenation novella; but the writing of *Gone With the Wind* – a long, painstaking and secretive activity – was Mitchell's attempt to exorcise conflicts and concerns within her own experience, and also to construct a comprehensive, representative epic of her region, class, race and sex. Significantly her only published fiction, the novel alludes to the conflicts of a wealthy Atlanta lawyer's daughter brought up to be a southern belle and debutante, increasingly uneasy with the decorous, insipid Junior League social world she was expected to join. It draws on its author's difficult girlhood of resistance to a strongly feminist, Catholic mother and stern, remote father; a passionate and irresponsible adolescence, followed by a disastrous marriage to a glamorous but decadent bootlegger. And it documents the family's fortunes both after the Civil War and also during the First World War, when Margaret Mitchell lost her fiancé in battle, and her family much property and wealth in a terrible fire caused by drought which (as Sherman had done fifty years earlier) destroyed a large part of the city.[7]

But of more significance for the present article is the way the novel attempts a strongly partisan, panoramic treatment of the white southern plantocracy, especially from the perspective of its women. Like their male counterparts, southern women from the late nineteenth century onwards have had a strong affinity with their region, and with their sectional history. Many of them came from close families which passed on stories and memories of previous generations, and since the Civil War those narratives have concerned the radical shifts and disruptions in social and family life, caused by political events post-1860. Margaret Mitchell was the latest in a long series of southern women to address themselves to a female/feminist fictional interpretation of the war and its aftermath.

Throughout the 1880s and 1890s, after the violent and divisive Reconstruction period, there was a national move for appeasement in the name of 'One Nation'; one form which this took was a new sympathetic interest by nothern publishers in the South and southern versions of recent historical events. Journalism and fiction about the southern states found a ready market in northern journals and presses, and many southern white women took up the challenge previously laid down by the famous abolitionist text *Uncle Tom's Cabin* and the dissenting texts of such southern critics as George Washington Cable, to present their sectional perspective to a national reading public. Now forgotten writers such as Sherwood Bonner, Ruth McEnery Stuart and Molly Moore Davis jumped on a fairly lucrative bandwagon, and catered for the vogue for 'local colour' stories and novels detailing southern regional characters, climates, customs and dialects. The most critically successful of these, Louisiana writer Grace King, began to write out of deep loyalty to her state and class. Like other white southern apologists, King was enraged by Cable's fictional and journalistic attacks on the South and especially its racial history. She wrote of her 'endeavor to call attention at least to some of those relations brought on by slavery, honorable to all concerned. It seems to me, white as well as black women have a sad showing in what some people call romance . . . as I recollect these things, I think I shall try to write them. . . . '8 This polemical project was shared by dozens of southern women writing during the last decades of the nineteenth century. And although with the new century, northern publishers lost interest in literature arguing a white supremacist, neo-Confederate case for the South, the 'Hell no, we ain't forgittin' southern line re-emerged in various kinds of discourse. Concern with the particular nature of the southern states and the neo-Confederate cause was experiencing something of a revival by the time Margaret Mitchell began to write. The 1930s were a period of renewed national interest in the South. President Roosevelt's identification of the South as the nation's primary economic problem led to considerable focus on the nature of its people and the character of the region. This attention came from different sources, such as social scientists (especially in the new centre for regional studies set up at the University of North Carolina); from the documents, statistics and photographs of the Farm Security Administration (FSA); and from Hollywood film-makers who produced a crop of movies with southern settings and themes, ranging from the antebellum melodramas *The Littlest Rebel* (Butler, 1935) and *Jezebel* (Wyler, 1938) to the sentimental and racist *Hallelujah!* (Vidor, 1929) and *Showboat* (Whale, 1936).

Several of these films were based on southern novels, and throughout the 1930s southern fiction enjoyed a minor vogue. Novelists such as William Faulkner and Ellen Glasgow, who had established themselves in the 1920s, consolidated their reputations throughout the 1930s. A Southern Renaissance was celebrated, and the decade saw the maturing or beginning careers of a remarkable number of southern poets and prose writers, many of them women – Caroline Gordon, Elizabeth Madox Roberts, Carson

McCullers and Eudora Welty among others. As a measure of the northern establishment's enthusiasm for southern materials, it is interesting to note the now-forgotten novel by Caroline Miller, *Lamb in His Bosom* (1933). To the surprise of critics, this first novel by an unknown southerner, a saga of white Georgian farmers from the revolutionary period to the mid-nineteenth century, was awarded the 1934 Pulitzer Prize and became a considerable bestseller. It was because he anticipated an exciting trend of southern writing that – like his predecessors in the 1880s and 90s – Harold Latham, vice-president of Macmillan, went South. After initially despairing of meeting any promising new writers, he was introduced to Margaret Mitchell; prising her manuscript from a very reluctant author, Latham realised its potential in a new market for southern materials, and rushed *Gone With the Wind* into print.

Margaret Mitchell's project in writing *Gone With the Wind* can be seen as a southern woman's version of a rising southern confidence and revived sense of dignity. When she said, in a speech to the Macon Writers Club, 'We must tell the truth, we writers of the South, we must give a true interpretation of our section, and so set our Southland right with the world,'[9] she was echoing the sentiments of other southerners who were busy doing just that in their works. A document which reflects that renewed sectionalism and southern assurance is the influential, though controversial collection of essays by twelve southern writers, *I'll Take My Stand*, published in pamphlet form in 1930. This collection argued that the task of southern (male) writers was to fight the Civil War all over again, 'affording a last stand in America against the industrial devourer'. The 'stand' which it declared they would take was in support of 'a Southern way of life against what may be called the American or prevailing way . . . [seen as the opposition] Agrarian *versus* Industrial'. The essays recall with pride and pleasure the Old South of (wealthy white) leisure and intelligence, which they see as having achieved 'a kind of imaginatively balanced life lived out in a definite social tradition'.[10] The adoption of agrarianism, its values derived from the Old South, is seen politically as a counter to the 'Communist menace' which would threaten the USA with advanced industrialism. One of the pamphlet's key authors, Robert Penn Warren, had wanted to entitle it *Tracts Against Communism*.

Margaret Mitchell also saw her writing as a counter to communism. She rejoiced in the attacks on *Gone With the Wind* from 'the Left Wingers' as she called them, since 'Everything about the book and the mind are abhorrent to all they believe in'.[11] She delighted in the Yugoslav press denunciation of the book because it deplored those elements of the novel she most prized, its 'glorification of individual courage and individual enterprise . . . the love of a person for their land and their home'.[12] And most significantly, she passionately defended her version of Black-white relations against the hostility of the Radical press which, she claimed, 'tried to use "Gone With the Wind" as a whip to drive the Southern Negroes into the Communist Party somewhat in the same manner that "Uncle Tom's Cabin" was used to recruit Abolitionists'.[13] This reference back to Harriet Beecher Stowe's *Uncle Tom's Cabin* acts as a reminder of the political significance of fictional texts in the ideological construction of the South and its racial history. For Mitchell certainly saw her own novel as a serious attempt to set straight distorted (non-southern) records, and to argue the neo-Confederate case. Much of her enormous body of correspondence on the subject of the novel consists of defences against charges of historical inaccuracy and inadequate research; ironically, like her ideological enemy Harriet Beecher Stowe, she spent much time citing documentary and anecdotal evidence to prove her version of southern history was accurate in every detail.

Margaret Mitchell had, after all, been brought up in a politically sophisticated but defensive city and family. Like other Georgia girls, she had been taught very young to sing Confederate songs like 'I'm a Good Old Rebel and That's What I am'; she attended numerous commemorative parades and rallies for war heroes; and spent long hours listening to anecdotes from family archives. She shared her parents' passion for Georgia's political history. But as her biographer Anne Edwards comments, 'She heard all there was to hear about the Civil War except that the Confederates had lost it.'[14]

There were indications of the future propagandist in the child Margaret's domestic dramatisation of the novel *The Traitor*. Its author, Thomas Dixon, one of the most reactionary and overtly racist of nineteenth century white apologists, wrote several novels about Reconstruction, including two specifically focusing on the Ku Klux Klan, *The Traitor* and *The Clansman* (1905, later to provide the basis of D.W. Griffith's film *The Birth of a Nation*, 1915). After the publication of *Gone With the Wind*, Dixon wrote Mitchell a letter of praise, saying he wished to write a study of the book. She responded in fulsome fashion, assuring him, 'I was practically raised on your books, and love them very much.'[15] She was also a great fan of the Griffith film; its huge success was almost certainly a spur to her own decision to chronicle the fortunes of postbellum southern families in an epic and romantic form.

Book and film record the horrors of the Civil War, and the even greater atrocities of Reconstruction, with carpetbagger government, the ministrations of the Freedmen's Bureau, and the introduction of Black legislators. Twentieth century historians have documented the far greater hardships of and violence towards Blacks than whites in that short period before southern Democrats re-imposed an even more repressive white racist rule; but Dixon and Griffith argue an uncritical white supremacist line, showing whites as victims of ruthless hordes of freedmen. The Freedmen's Bureau, set up by Congress to supervise the transition of Blacks from slavery to freedom in terms of labour relations, the law, medical care and education, is portrayed as malevolent and destructive: *Birth of a Nation* calls it 'the charity of a generous North misused to delude the ignorant'. Blacks are either loyal darkies or they are greedy, grasping, insolent beasts who as state legislators eat and drink with feet on the desk, and gang-rape white women. Whites are repeatedly seen as 'helpless' in the face of 'crazed Negroes'; especially after the rape of a young girl who commits suicide, the Ku Klux Klan is seen as the only organisation fit to save the South from anarchic Black rule.

It is important not to underestimate the influence of *The Birth of a Nation* during the 1920s and 1930s. *The Clansman*, from which the film was adapted, came out in 1905 at a time when racial feelings were running high and southern racists were reaching an increasingly wide national audience. Between 1900 and the year *The Birth of a Nation* appeared, Dixon's trilogy on what he called 'the race conflict' was among a series of books and public lectures characterising Blacks as degraded, bestial and beyond redemption – with titles such as 'The Negro a Beast' and *The Negro, A Menace to American Civilization*. These culminated in southern educator Thomas Pearce Bailey's 'racial creed of the Southern people', which argued for white domination, Teutonic race purity, no social or political equality for the inferior Negro, and the rights of the South to settle the Negro question in its own way.[16] Such texts were consistent with a new national support for racist ideologies, and voiced a now fashionable southern nostalgia for that period of vengeance on carpetbag government, the 'Redemption' of a white Democrat South.

Dixon's trilogy was an enormous popular success. When a dramatised version of *The Clansman* (dedicated, incidentally, to his uncle, 'Grand Titan of the Invisible Empire Ku Klux Klan') was shown in Atlanta in 1905, it attracted large audiences; the following year, in a city which had previously seen much victimisation of Black citizens, there was a violent race riot. The film version, first shown as *The Clansman* on 1 January 1915, was also instantly successful; soon renamed *The Birth of a Nation, or The Clansman*, it was to become regarded as a triumphant landmark in the history of popular film. Ominously, and surely not coincidentally, 1915 saw another significant event: the rededication of the Ku Klux Klan on Stone Mountain, Georgia, with the establishment of its Imperial Palace on Peachtree Street (not only the street where Margaret Mitchell lived and worked as a journalist, but also that on which her fictional Rhett Butler built a grand house for his bride, Scarlett). By the mid 1920s, the Klan had re-established itself firmly in both southern and national life; the Atlanta headquarters boasted it was the capital to six million Klansmen. In the early 1920s, there was a virtual reign of terror within Atlanta, with Blacks watching in horror as their churches, farms and businesses went up in flames. The fear of lynching kept many cowering at home – including Margaret Mitchell's family servants. A decade later, the 1933 Payne Report stated that Griffith's racism had been a major influence on children. And when one examines the adulation heaped on both racist, white supremacist films *Birth of a Nation* and *Gone With the Wind*, one might say that where Griffith left off in the early 1930s, Mitchell and her novel/film took over, and still carry enormous influence.

The political project of *Gone With the Wind* is hammered home in the strident tones familiar to readers of southern fiction and fans of southern movies of the 1930s.[17] While the first volume is careful to demonstrate southerners' ambivalence and varying degrees of commitment to the Confederacy and the human sacrifice of the Civil War, the second volume becomes overtly polemical and unashamedly partisan. The central characters express private or public doubts about Secession and fighting for the 'Cause': Ashley Wilkes's letters home from battle express extreme disillusionment with the war, and Rhett Butler scorns to fight a war he knows the Confederacy cannot win, in favour of profitable blockade-running. Scarlett herself wonders whether all the destruction of human lives and property can be justified. But as Reconstruction begins, so the tone changes; Margaret Mitchell intrudes long passages of vitriolic description of carpetbag and Negro governments, reiterating the ingratitude and 'insolence' of 'nigger judges, nigger legislators – black apes out of the jungle' (p.630), and the degradation of 'innocent', 'helpless', 'crushed' whites – that humiliated 'royalty in exile' (p.593) so eulogised by her southern fictional predecessors. As with other neo-Confederate writers, Mitchell uses Reconstruction as the great unifying and consolidating historical crisis for southern whites. While the war divides and destroys families, breaking down traditional class, gender and race relations, Reconstruction restores white southern confidence in its own rightness and infallibility. Thus Ashley becomes active in the Ku Klux Klan; southern madonna Melanie, realist New Woman Scarlett and whore-with-a-heart-of-gold Belle

Watling conspire to protect their Klansmen; and hero Rhett Butler suffers no social stigma after imprisonment for killing a Black man who was rude to a white lady. The text argues overtly and implicitly that the South has suffered enough, and that its vengeance on the Negro race is understandable and valid.

The most powerful way in which the Lost Cause is vindicated is through the apostasy of Rhett Butler; the cold cynic of the early war years, he abandons Scarlett on the road to Tara in order to join the Confederate army, a sentimental gesture which is shown to derive from his deepest sectional loyalty to 'our fair Southland' (p.381). And while his quixotic and outrageous manner remains (unlike true southern gentlemen he makes a notoriously large fortune during the war and Reconstruction), he comes to realise he is at heart a 'true Southerner'. His last words on leaving Scarlett are legendary; but when he says he doesn't 'give a damn' what happens to her, he is rejecting more than one woman. For the reformed rake also tells her he is leaving Atlanta because it is 'too raw . . . too new' – terms associated throughout the text with both Scarlett and that new cosmopolitan city buoyed up by Yankee capital and new immigration. New South and New Woman are equally repugnant. A tired Rhett Butler, once scallawag, blockade-runner and dandy, is off in humble search of 'old' values – 'the clannishness of families, honour and security, roots that go deep . . . the genial grace of days that are gone' (p.1008). He has been won round by all those elements of southern life which the Yankee and the freedman have destroyed and devalued; the conservative retreat of this sadder and wiser romantic hero speaks the political sub-text of the whole novel. As in *I'll Take My Stand*, the antebellum South, controlled by a white ruling class which (in the nicest possible way . . .) dominated its own faithful slaves, comes to represent a number of eternal, fixed, enduring truths which are defined as family loyalty, gentility, continuity and, most important, female subordination. No wonder so many of the New Women of the 1930s wrote anxiously to Margaret Mitchell asking if she thought Rhett would ever return.

And what of Scarlett O'Hara? Named after the Irish Scarletts who fought for a free Ireland, she offers the reader/audience many a *frisson* of possible roles and choices derived from Old and New South, confusions of gender and race, and historical and mythological frames of reference. Of all the characters in the novel, Scarlett most embodies the dramatic shifts and reversals in postbellum economic and social relations in the South. Treated when young like the son her father never had, she 'found the road to ladyhood hard' (p.60), a distinct advantage when the war makes a mockery of the ideology of frail, innocent southern femininity. Losing her mother, and finding herself the head of a household because her father is deranged and incapable, Scarlett becomes the man of the family. Organising food and cotton production on the ruined plantation, she assumes her father's role, and is recognised as patriarchal substitute by all the men with whom she comes into contact; single-handedly she makes Tara once more economically and socially viable. The novel confirms the appropriateness of Scarlett's gender reversal through emphasising a repugnance towards her own sexuality and child-bearing, and her inadequacy as a mother to the three children she unwillingly bears and rears. Furthermore, it is the inherited strength and earthiness of her Irish *father* which saves her from the pusillanimity of the inbred, aristocratic and feminised Wilkes clan who in adversity come to depend so heavily on her. And it is that very rejection of femininity which fascinates Rhett Butler; he alone sees clearly that she is 'no lady', and identifies with her as social outcast and deviant: 'We are not gentlemen and we have no honour. . . . We are both scoundrels' (pp.916–17)

This is irresistible to the feminist or reluctantly feminine reader, whose uneasy relationship to her own gender position and male-defined female sexuality must strike many chords with Scarlett's situation. And it is Scarlett's transformation which appears to be so memorable for women readers; we fantasise about role-swapping and gender confusion which will not only mature and strengthen us, but will make us both independent and utterly irresistible to a raffish and dominating romantic hero (who won't mind if we bolt our whisky neat in a practised manner). But as I suggested earlier, it is important for us to be aware of the political implications of this emotional identification – especially when a text is reinforcing class and race relations and assumptions we find repugnant. For *Gone With the Wind* plays not only on the fascination of gender confusion, but also on those threatening class and race reversals which test Scarlett and, by association, the female reader.

When Scarlett returns to the remains of Tara after Sherman's devastating march through Georgia, she has to confront the necessity of working with her own hands, or starving to death. At first she is horrified by the implications of starting from scratch: 'Me? Pick cotton? . . . Like a field hand? Like white trash?' (p.438). And in case the reader is in danger of seeing her as unforgivably fastidious, Mitchell also emphasises the horror of Mammy and the other 'family' Blacks at the dissolution of class distinctions. With 'a caste feeling even stronger than her own', Mammy, Pork and Prissy object to working in the fields: 'They reiterated that they were house niggers, not field hands. Mammy, in particular, declared vehemently that she had never ever been a yard nigger. She had been born in the Robillard great house, not in the quarters. . . . (p.445)'. All the whites and Blacks are appalled at the thought of the family's former overseer (now working for the Freedmen's Bureau) buying Tara, getting his hands on the Robillard silver, and even bringing Negroes to live there.

But it is Scarlett who embodies the spirit of a revitalised postbellum southern womanhood/post 1930s Depression (white) southern grit. She resolves never to be hungry again, and fights to restore the position and confidence of her class while agreeing to small compromises en route (compromises the Blacks and more traditional 'aristocratic' whites are unprepared to make). She sends the family and former house-slaves to till the land, and she accepts a poor white 'cracker' as her sister's husband. Most significantly, she is prepared to become the sort of woman she has been raised to abominate: playing the whore for Rhett Butler in jail – dressing alluringly in Tara's curtains in an unsuccessful attempt to persuade him to pay her taxes; and for Frank Kennedy, who is lured into marrying her and paying the taxes to ensure Tara stays O'Hara. Belle Watling, Rhett's mistress, is a constant presence in the Atlanta scenes of the novel, acting to remind Scarlett and the white reader of the desperate conditions into which southern white women were driven by Reconstruction; the pure blushing Melanie Wilkes breaks social taboos by accepting money for the Confederate cause from Miss Watling, while Rhett emphasises the new flexible class mobility by comparing Scarlett and Belle as shrewd businesswomen (p.921). Scarlett, then, embodies all those transformations of planter-class white women in the first decades after the war: she must play the roles of patriarch, canny businesswoman and landowner, and also (since her capital is mainly invested in her body) of whore. And all this to ensure that land – that signifier of white dominance – remains in the 'right' hands.

But even more potentially disruptive and degrading than all these new roles is the most tabooed of all, the equation of white Scarlett O'Hara with her own slaves or freed Blacks in general. A common analogy in late nineteenth century fiction by southern white women, this dissolution of difference between white and Black is used continually to point up the tragic impact of the war and Reconstruction on southern whites whom, like Ashley Wilkes, 'God intended . . . to sit in a great house, talking with pleasant people, playing the piano . . . ' (p.512). It is also used to celebrate that immense courage and heroism of white southern *women* who played such a major ideological and political role in reasserting racial difference, ensuring that the white South did indeed rise again.

In *Gone With the Wind*, the rather titillating and appealing gender confusions experienced by Scarlett are balanced by ominous suggestions of mingled racial identities. However uneasily feminine, Scarlett is indisputably white. As with other southern heroines, that whiteness is emphasised throughout the novel – from her magnolia-white skin to her small white hands (contrasted as they are with the 'huge black paws' of the family slaves, p.299). But once the war and abolition have hit Tara, oh-so-white Scarlett is in danger of losing her dominant racial status. On the road back to Tara, she sleeps in the wagon 'like a field hand on hard planks' (p.385), and once back on the plantation, works on the land knowing she would 'never feel like a lady again until her table was weighted with silver and crystal and smoking with rich food . . . until black hands and not white took the cotton from Tara' (p.594). After the fire in the kitchen, Scarlett and Melanie laugh at each other's blackened faces, Melanie likening her friend's to 'the end man in a minstrel show' (p.459); and when Scarlett in her finery visits Rhett in jail, it is her blistered, red hands which show him that, far from idling, she's been 'working like a nigger' (p.564). This motif of the blackening of white skin, hence name and status, acts to exhort the reader to deplore the Confederacy's defeat, and to vindicate the violent tactics of the Ku Klux Klan and other southern whites to redeem that white supremacy which is sanctified as natural within the narrative.

There is a significant difference between *Gone With the Wind* and other romantic novels – namely, the happy ending involves not a man but a piece of property/land. While Rhett departs, declaring indifference to his wife, surprisingly Scarlett does not do what we all ache for – pursue him to bring about a final tempestuous reconciliation. No, the novel ends in a manner inconsistent with True Romances but entirely appropriate for the political and historical project to which the novel addresses itself throughout. Scarlett decides to return to the 'sheltering walls' of Tara in order to 'plan her campaign' of retrieving Rhett Butler. The thought of Tara comforts and strengthens her, and gives her renewed confidence in herself and her ability to do what she's always done – get a man on whom she's set her mind.

Her Irish father's home Tara is significantly named after the sacred place of early Celtic Ireland, the supreme seat of the monarch.[18] In Irish mythology, land is described in terms of a woman's form; until the seventeenth century the land was imagined in terms of a woman old as the hills, restored endlessly to youth through union with the right mate. Woman earth outlives men and tribes; in Irish mythology women allow power to kings through a sexual/supernatural union. Thus it is fitting for Scarlett to return finally to Tara – as mythic natural home of woman, where she may both survive and be reborn, and also lure back and reconquer her king. Hence the militaristic language associated with the plantation – it is a virtual fortress from which Scarlett had once before 'emerged . . . strong and armed for victory' (p.1010). And hence the symbolic resonance of Tara on which the David Selznick film lingers: repeating as a refrain the silhouetted figure of Scarlett/Woman against red sky, dark Tara/Mythological Haven or Stronghold, heightened by the swelling chords of Max Steiner's theme music.

But Tara is not (as in Irish mythology) defined simply as a female haven, a woman's place. It is explicitly a place for *upper middle class white women*, a site existing timelessly outside real social relations, and all class and race divisions and conflicts of interest. Tara is the embodiment of southern white femininity: the white-walled and white-curtained house and 'fleecy white' cotton bolls contrast reassuringly with the red earth, green pines and bushes. And most of all with the Blackness of Mammy, who of course 'would be there'. Scarlett's final longing is for the 'broad bosom on which to lay her head, the gnarled black hand on her hair', for it is only within Mammy's mute embrace that Scarlett can reassert her secure, dominant position in class and race terms: 'Mammy, the last link with the old days.' Scarlett is thus revived by the thought of Mammy, and the anticipated reconnection with her antebellum heritage, confirmed now by the return to Tara. The final page of the novel brings together into a metaphoric and symbolic harmony a naturalised vision of a reborn South, safely in the hands of strong, capable, property-owning white women, vindicated and supported by the passive, loving 'endurance' of Black womanhood which knows its (subordinate) place.

It is salutary to recall James Baldwin's view of the 'rust-red earth of Georgia' which Scarlett O'Hara so eagerly reclaims as her own. He writes of his thoughts as he looks out of a plane window at this earth: 'I could not suppress the thought that this earth had acquired its color from the blood that dripped down from these trees. My mind was filled with the image of a Black man . . . hanging from a tree, while white men watched him and cut his sex from him with a knife.'[19] In Margaret Mitchell's novel, the blood-red earth is a warm and womb-like land where white and Black show each other mutual devotion and loyalty, but only outside postbellum historical realities, and within a cavalier plantation myth of prelapsarian personal relations. Thus the conclusion of *Gone With the Wind* speaks not only of one woman's triumph over adversity and suffering (the way most readers have taken it) but also of an unrepentant and defiant neo-Confederate spirit which – like *I'll Take My Stand* – wages the Civil War beyond Reconstruction, Redemption, into 1936 and well into our own time. 'With the spirit of her people who would not know defeat', the finally optimistic Scarlett plans her return to Mammy, that Aunt Jemima fantasy figure of white imagination, epitomising/constructing as it does 'the ultimate sexist–racist vision of ideal black womanhood – complete submission to the will of whites . . . who embodied solely those characteristics they as colonizers wished to exploit'.[20]

I began by emphasising that *Gone With the Wind* has been sensationally successful, and in its novel and film versions stands as an extraordinary twentieth century phenomenon, a familiar and much loved part of popular culture. I have also argued that, unique as it is in some ways, in others it is very typical of a whole body of nineteenth and early twentieth century southern fiction, and shares with several different discourses specific ideological and political positions which a defensive South adopted strongly in the 1920s and 1930s. In a decade of the Depression, the New Deal, and urgent national and international political and sectional divisions and conflicts, its idealised version of an organic, harmonious Old South of agrarian, fixed values had (and indeed still has) considerable popular appeal. And I have suggested that it is the anachronistic, reactionary and racist connotations of just such a mythic South which make both novel and film politically dangerous.

It is hard not to sound like a puritanical killjoy; after all, the book is a damned good read, the film a marvellous, stunning production. But in relation to romance, white feminists are both vulnerable and guilty. While in the early days of the women's movement we concealed evidence of our pleasure in romantic novels and weepie films, there is now a massive coming-out of romance freaks. In some ways, of course, this is progressive, since it takes seriously women's real frustrations and desires which romance alone can address and in some measure satisfy. But we must beware that our populist enthusiasm does not blind us to the potentially reactionary and divisive implications of some romantic fiction. And when we read the damning accounts, by Angela Davis, bell hooks and Alice Walker, of that racist white feminism which has alienated Black women from the recent women's movement, we have to think again before recuperating for celebration racist texts-we-have-loved, as well as before going in Scarlett O'Hara rags to the feminist ball.

Notes

1 R.M. Brownstein, *Becoming a Heroine: Reading About Women in Novels*, Harmondsworth, Penguin, 1984, p.7.
2 Bob Light and John Houston, 'Neither Washington nor Moscow, but International Socialism'.

3 A. Goodwyn Jones, *Tomorrow is Another Day: The Woman Writer in the South, 1859–1936*, Baton Rouge, Louisiana State University Press, 1981.

4 T. Morrison, *Song of Solomon*, London, Triad/Panther, 1980, p.84.

5 A. Walker, *You Can't Keep a Good Woman Down*, London, The Women's Press, 1982, p.118.

6 R. Bromley, 'Natural boundaries: the social function of popular fiction', *Red Letters*, no. 7, 1977, p.36.

7 For the most reliable biographical information, see A. Edwards, *The Road to Tara: The Life of Margaret Mitchell*, London, Hodder & Stoughton, 1983.

8 Grace King, Letter to Charles D. Warner, 17 September, 1885, Grace King Papers, Dept of Archives and Manuscripts, Louisiana State University, Baton Rouge.

9 Quoted in M. Elder Jones, 'Me and my book', *Georgia Review*, No. 16, Spring 1962, p.186.

10 Twelve Southerners, *I'll Take My Stand: The South and the Agrarian Tradition*, Baton Rouge, Louisiana State University Press, 1980, pp.xliv and 60.

11 Margaret Mitchell, Letter to Stark Young, 29 September 1936, in R. Harwell, ed., *Margaret Mitchell's Gone With the Wind Letters 1936–1949*, New York, Macmillan, 1976, p.66.

12 Margaret Mitchell, Letter to Governor James M. Cox, 28 July 1949, in Harwell, op. cit., p.425.

13 Margaret Mitchell, Letter to Susan Myrick, 17 April 1939, in Harwell, op. cit., p.273.

14 Edwards, op. cit., p.23.

15 Margaret Mitchell, Letter to Thomas Dixon, 15 August 1936, in Harwell, op. cit., p.52.

16 See C. Van Woodward, *Origins of the New South 1877–1913*, Baton Rouge, Louisiana State University Press, 1951, pp.350–6.

17 The edition of the novel to which I refer is M. Mitchell, *Gone With the Wind*, London, Pan, 1974. Specific page references to this edition will be given in parenthesis.

18 See Proinsias MacCana, 'Women in Irish mythology', *Crane Bag*, vol.4, May 1980, p.7. I am very grateful to Claire Johnston for this reference.

19 J. Baldwin, 'Nobody knows my name: a letter from the South', in *Nobody Knows My Name: More Notes of a Native Son*, New

York, Dell, 1961, p.87.
20 b. hooks, *Ain't I a Woman: Black Women and Feminism*, London, Pluto, 1981, p.84.

Publicity still from Associated British Picture Corporation's film of *The Franchise Affair*, 1950

7
Writing fictions: femininity and the 1950s

ALISON LIGHT

As a postgraduate student looking at women's writing in the 1950s, I was not surprised to discover that both women and their writing are conspicious by their glaring absence from most social historical and literary critical accounts of the era. This is the starting point for much feminist research, though it is none the less crippling and appalling in its effects. But perhaps I found this absence all the more shocking given the comparative recentness of the period – after all we know that women *were* there because some of *us* were! Probably many readers of this chapter have some kind of memory or image of the 1950s based on their own experience, so that these new accounts of a time one has actually lived through dramatically illustrate how quickly women are written out of history. And they remind us too that one of the most, if not *the* most powerful construction of history, the making of a past, is in the activity of writing. Working on the material of recent periods, particularly those within living memory, throws the problems and delights of being a 'historian' into fascinating relief. The 1950s offer an enormous range of accessible sources so where does the process of selection start? Perhaps if we can think about those processes of history-in-the-making it can help us push further at the question of its political effects. In other words, looking at the 1950s brought me up against history as text, or textuality, as something which is endlessly written and re-written with all the concomitant questions of authorship and audience – who writes it and for whom? And then follows the even bigger question, how far is this 'history' only ever 'ideology', an imaginary representation of people's lives, and what relation does it bear to those lives as they are lived?

So I started my research with the basic question, 'where *were* women in the 1950s?' And I found that this was further complicated by the characterisation of those years, by commentators on the right and on the left, as a period of 'middle class consensus'. Very crudely, in social-historical terms, the 1950s are seen as moving from the austerity of the immediate post-war period (usually dated from 1945 to 1953 or thereabouts), from the exigencies of rationing, the slow recovery of the wartime economy, through to the boom of capitalist industry in the mid-1950s, bringing with it full employment and the optimism of increasing prosperity. And three successive Tory governments. Most standard historical accounts[1] see it as a time, then, of consensus, of the reconstruction and consolidation of the social order, as it realigned itself beneath the values of a powerful and growing middle class. The relative agreement of the political parties over policy, for example over welfarism, was captured in the coining of the term 'Butskellism'[2], whilst the long, stable sweep of the Macmillan governments, and its dream of affluence for all, has stayed with us in the catchphrase of the 1959 election: 'you've never had it so good.'

Most analyses then go on to foreground the emergence of a new class fraction in the decade: the white-collar men of the industrial boom and of consumerism – managers, advertisers, estate agents and so forth. How the accompanying social mobility is viewed depends, of course, on the allegiances of the historian. Yet few of these histories include more than a token reference to women's work and almost no discussion of their social and political relation to any ideology of consensus.

Whilst these economic models of class remain especially exclusive of discussions of women's positions in the 1950s, feminist historians have begun to put women back on that map via the debates around sexuality itself. The work of writers like Elizabeth Wilson, Jeffrey Weeks and Denise Riley have begun to draw out the ways in which the family and, more critically, femininity becomes one of the central pivots of post-war reconstruction within social policy and welfarism in particular.[3] It seems that a renewed emphasis on a normative homogenising femininity, that was to seek its sexual and social fulfilment almost entirely within the confines of marriage and the home, re-emerges as part of that 'middle class consensus' with a force and uniformity which one might associate more with the demands of the 1850s than with those of a century later. Ideologies of family life, newly significant after the disruption of the war, sought to re-situate women firmly back within the traditional roles of wifedom and motherhood. The glory of this re-enshrinement was effectively symbolised by images of the new young Queen and her growing family. Discourses on child care, parental responsibility, the burgeoning of family planning and marital advice clinics, together with a number of government commissions on family life, all evidence the centrality of gender to that construction of an ideology of social reconciliation.

Yet what about feminism itself? What was women's relation to this ideological onslaught? The immediate post-war period appears to have allowed some challenging of traditional roles, but what became of the energy with which women engaged in, say, the campaigns for nursery provision in the 1940s? Did women truly welcome that return to the bosom of the family and march off gaily to the baby clinics, Doctor Spock in one hand and Farley's Rusks in the other? And how does this tally with the increasing numbers of women, especially married women, who entered or stayed in employment after the war? Is it helpful to generalise about 'femininity' across the class divisions which necessitated very different familial roles? How do we begin to chart the more subtle gradations of change within the period which might speak to the contradictory relations between what women lived and experienced and the official descriptions of, or prescriptions for, their lives? If protest, however partial, did exist, is it simply, like so much of women's experience, not yet recorded in 'history'? Or if, as it seems, many women settled for some version of familial ideology, what did it have to offer them that was real and important, pleasurable as well as con- straining within that consensus? Perhaps another advantage in looking at such a recent period of history is that one has to drop the people-were-more-stupid- in-the-past-and-now-we-know-better approach to history; many of our own choices – or those of our mothers and fathes – are clearly implicated, and thus the question 'what did it feel like to live through those changes?' cannot be so easily dismissed as naive or irrelevant.

It seemed to me that if I were asking questions about gendered 'subjectivity' and history, then literary dis- course might well be one place where the contradictions and tensions of women's lives were explored. Literature, and in particular the novel, has long provided a space for middle class women to imagine and re-cast the concerns of their gendered existence – romantic love, sexual relations, marriage, the family and property.

And yet in turning to literary critical histories of the 1950s I drew an even more peculiar kind of blank.

Whilst there are still a sad few who wish to offer us a literary heritage of a hundred best novels dominated by such luminaries as William Golding, Evelyn Waugh and C.P. Snow, even these commentators are inclined to lament the death of Great Art and mark the end of Modern Literature in roundabout 1930. This itself is a sign of the impact made by the shifts in the class of readers and writers that took place on a large scale in the post-war period. Most literary critical establishments have had to admit the effect of those 'Angry Young Men' – Wain, Amis, Osborne and later writers like Braine, Barstow and Sillitoe – and in doing so to expose the supposedly universal values and appeal of literary texts to some kind of class analysis. This opening up has been no less important for all that these *enfants terribles* have largely drifted rightwards and ended up in the very middle class establishments they began by attacking.[4] But the emphasis on class has still been a predominantly masculine one whose full implications have by no means been taken up. My first year of research at Sussex University, for example, was a twentieth century literature MA in which this radical alternative to endlessly revisiting Brideshead was being (with some resistance) offered. However much they are now in danger of becoming a 'canon', *Lucky Jim*, *Look Back in Anger*, *Room at The Top*, and *Saturday Night and Sunday Morning* must all raise the issue of class, and do therefore constitute a very real threat to those who would rather not discuss how texts come to be designated literature in the first place, who reads them, reviews them, what gets taught and how. That said, I was still left with the rather bizarre impression, which left-wing lit. crit. does little to unsettle, that women and sexuality (the two tend to go together) did not get to be on the literary agenda until the 1960s.

The major concerns of those texts – class mobility, consumerism, the final collapse of British imperial power – tend to be treated as somehow separate and separable from those of gender and sexual difference. Yet one look at the kinds of images of femininity in, say, Jimmy Porter's attack on middle class complacency, shows it to be saturated with, and most often *expressed through*, a bleak and brutal misogyny. From the hilarious anti-intellectualism of *Lucky Jim* to the resigned opportunism of *Room at The Top*, all these texts proclaim a different class of masculinity at the expense of a degraded femininity. Whatever is going on in these texts, surely it isn't the relegation of the sexual to the somehow 'larger' issues of the state or the public sphere, but rather a dramatic statement of their interdependence?[5]

So that gives you some idea of where I came in; these are still, I believe, the dominant constructions of history and literature, the layers of knowledges which map out and limit the terrain within which it becomes possible to talk about either the 'fifties' or women writing in them. In asking 'where were women in the 1950s?', a socialist feminist analysis has to acknowledge these dominant constructions of the period as marking out sites of real and effective power. It is not a case, then, of looking for Angry Young Women who will simply make a nonsense of any understanding of the 1950s in terms of middle class hegemony; we need analyses, nevertheless, which will show how that hegemony was always having to be reproduced, that ideology of consensus re-secured, *as* ideology, only ever bearing an imaginary relation to the dissonant and different existences it inscribed. It is here that I think literary texts can be used as a kind of wedge and it is in these terms that I am trying to think about the positions from which women wrote and read in that decade.

The main problem for feminists, then, with these literary and historical discourses has been that familiar one of a division into the public and the private spheres which continues to organise our labour and our knowledges, with the relegation of women (and with them sexuality) to the latter. It is the so-called public world of institiutions, workplaces, the legal and administrative apparatuses of the state that have chiefly constituted the field of history, particularly in its Marxist variety, whilst it is in opposition to this (but still within the terms of that binary division) that alternatives have been set up – oral history, for example, or that of 'marginalised' groups. Within the discourse of literary studies (of University English), on the other hand, that opposition has worked the other way round: Marxist and cultural studies, with their foregrounding of the economic and material conditions which determine literary production, have provided a vital corrective to the traditional view of literature as private and personal, belonging to the interior world of the individual emotions and expressivity. But in both cases the opposition of terms remains and needs, I think, in any feminist analysis, to be taken issue with. Not because feminism seeks to reinvest 'the personal' with a more unique status (sequestering ourselves yet again in the backwaters of bourgeois bliss), but in order to insist that the construction of gendered subjectivities – how we come to think of and live out our recognition of sexual differences – is not somehow separable from the demands of a larger public sphere, a sphere we then nominate 'the social'. Those subject-ivities are, precisely, *social*, equally the material and the means of 'history'. What feminism has brought to theories of social organisation, an emphasis on the centrality of sexual differentiation, has surely worked to dissolve these inadequate polarities, and to argue that no analysis which simply reproduces that bourgeois division of labour can ever fully understand or account for human existence or social change.[6]

Literary texts as historical evidence have tended then to be discussed in two ways: either, traditionally as the products of unique and solitary imaginations and biographies (which paradoxically are able to offer universal truths) or as social documents reflecting or being determined by a distinct and external social 'real'. I would like us to reconsider literature as an imaginative and fantastic medium, where fantasy, the fictionalisation of self, is not seen to be at odds with or simply in reaction to the social, but crucial to the living and the shaping of it. How can we think about literature as a *simultaneously* intimate and social, private and public practice, enmeshing and re-defining the boundaries between 'history' and 'subjectivity'? This seems to me to be where the language and interests of the discourse of psychoanalysis might come in, though I shall do little more here than gesture towards it. What psychoanalytic theory might be seen as usefully offering historians and literary critics alike is a recognition that *subjectivities* are indeed socially organised and lived. Further, in thinking about literary texts as fantasies, the psychoanalytic notion of the unconscious opens up an exploration of writing as *both* a restatement of and a resistance to the definitions and demands of gender.[7] Literary texts written from and read by subjectivities which are never wholly unified or fully conscious dramatise the transversing of a web of possible identities and selves which are imaginable only at certain times and within certain social or cultural organisations. If we ask what relation women had to those dominant ideologies of femininity in the 1950s then we have to explore the subjectivities organised discursively within and across literary texts as profoundly gendered. For if literary discourse permits and embodies an imaginary reformulation and re-definition of 'the social', whose selectivity betrays both the conscious and unconscious desires of its subjects, then these desires may be seen to be differently organised and expressed for women and for men.

I would like us to consider ways of articulating the production in literary texts of gendered subjectivities within and through those other historical discourses which go to make up 'a sense of self', like, for example, those of class or race. We need an analysis of the ways in which literatures offer fantasised resolutions and refusals of dominant gender definitions, together with an attention to literary texts as one of the central places in culture where such definitions are both formed and fought for. Such analyses deal as much with what is at stake in the pleasures of reading and of re-reading fictions as with the making and sharing of them. As we read back into the 1950s a two-way process is taking place, one which is both historically determined and determining; for it is not just that we cannot understand the novels of the period without reference to other discourses of femininity outside the literary, but also that we cannot fully understand the meanings and operations of those discourses without looking too at the part played by literary culture in the construction of sexual ideologies, and in the defining and regulating of the myriad femininities which come to be lived. Literature, and more especially novels of all kinds, have been a crucial arena for women in the formation and expression – the defining and playing out – of a middle class sexuality. Precisely because of its relegation to the 'private', and its practice as largely domestic labour, novel writing in British culture has been a unique and deeply pleasurable resource for (predominantly) bourgeois women in the last two hundred years; it has offered a route for both readers and writers into a different terrain within a culture

where they mostly exist in the imaginary representations of men. As I have suggested, this access has
been bought at the risk of their ghettoisation, the
devaluing of their work as 'other', personal and
private, wholly sexually determined or explained by
'femininity' itself.[8] Whilst not wanting yet again to
reassert 'femininity' and 'masculinity' as fixed poles
and wholly explanatory categories, I want to suggest
that femininity and masculinity be seen nevertheless as
prolifically rich and resonant in all texts and histories,
endlessly productive, keying into and interpreting the
regimes and meanings of those other available
discourses and sources of identity and power.

Perhaps we might think of novels as areas of
negotiation and exchange between, for example,
gender and class as they continually define and limit
each other: an exchange which is bounded by, but
never finally fixed within, the dominant definitions of
both.

Thus it is that in unravelling the ways in which the
dominant bourgeois femininity comes to be tested,
realigned, shored up and even simultaneously rejected
in the texts of the 1950s, a socialist feminist intervention can be made across a range of literary
material – 'highbrow', 'popular' or whatever. It is
worth noting too that the questions of audience and
reception are particularly complex in relation to
women and their patterns of reading. This is so when
we consider the number of women in the vast and
rambling audiences of library and magazine readership,
or the ritualised exchanges of romance fiction, for
example, where one novel may do the rounds of
several women readers: determining what constitutes
'popular' fiction in the 1950s is less than straightforward. Indeed hundreds of the bestsellers of the
1950s are *still* bestsellers – Monica Dickens, Daphne du
Maurier, Mary Stewart, Anya Seton, and Jean Plaidy,

to name but five authors; I think it is hard to underestimate the importance of the pleasures of reading fiction in many women's lives. I for one can clearly remember being directed to many of these authors by my mother at the Carnegie library on Saturday afternoons, and that many of my most impressive and delightful fantasies were evolved and lived through those fictions. For perhaps the special centrality of literary culture in our lives makes one thing plain: it continues to speak to us and for us if only because it is here that the meanings and pleasures of sexual difference are taken seriously for what they are – social dramas of the self.

I want now to turn to one 'popular' text written shortly after the war: *The Franchise Affair* by Josephine Tey, published in 1948. I want briefly to gesture at the ways in which feminine subjectivities come to be positioned and worked out in that text, in relation to the demands of a dominant bourgeois consensus over the proper social and sexual place of women. I intend, in particular, to examine its narrative organisation, and to point up how its definitions of class difference function both to express and contain sexual differences. Whilst such definitions locate the text firmly in its historical moment, the work which the narrative must perform in order to secure them, the shifts and jolts of the text, those very places which may appear as defects when the novel is judged according to the traditional criteria of 'realism' – these are the crucial areas for attention. It is here that the text reveals the effort with which it barely manages and sustains the definitions of class and gender difference. Thus it demonstrates their perilous insecurity *even* as the pleasure of the text may lie in effacing the contradictions between the demands of class and gender, their fraught dialectic. To begin to understand the symbolic satisfactions and appeal of such narratives, to chart the positions offered to the reader in the dynamics of the process of 'identification', is perhaps to gain some insight into the historical process itself: to glimpse a re-enactment, a staging of the parts played by class and gender in the construction of our subjectivities which see us all 'living within ideology' whilst simultaneously being always able to resist and re-define its terms.

Tey's novel is a 'thriller', a detective story with elements of the Gothic and of romance fiction. The plot revolves around the task of Robert Blair, a middle-aged country lawyer who turns detective in order to defend two local women against a seemingly bizarre slander: Marion Sharpe and her elderly mother are accused by a 15-year-old schoolgirl of keeping her locked up in the attic of their country house, the Franchise, alternately beating and starving her in the attempt to force her to be their maid. The girl's evidence, including some vivid bruises, seems at the beginning of the novel to be irrefutable; Blair, however, intrigued by the unconventional, 40-year-old Marion, sets out to prove the girl a liar. This is indeed what, after a long series of investigations which take Blair all over the post-war countryside, she turns out to be. The novel thus works by a reversal of our expectations, ending with the 'revelation' (by this time the only possibility) of the rampant sexuality which lurks beneath the demure grammar school girl's exterior, and with the reinstatement of the Sharpes. For it is essential to the narrative that the Sharpes don't fit into the local provincial society; they live, both literally and symbolically, on the margins of Milford, the small and mainly middle class Midlands town where the novel is set. The Sharpes are known as eccentrics who live apart in slightly sinister seclusion, refusing to join in the life of the community and not doing 'normal' things like holding coffee mornings or running jumble sales. The narrative follows two parallel lines of sexual and class inversion. From a position in which the girl, Betty Kane, is apparently the class victim of a pathologically warped spinster and her mother, we are brought to a position at the end of the novel in which the older women are restored to middle class grace and their sexual eccentricities (no husbands) forgiven; their vindication depends however on the parallel process – the discovery that the middle class Betty Kane is *really* from a 'deprived' working class background. Importantly, their triumph and the process of their embourgeoisment (however partial) can only be achieved at the expense of the young girl's degradation: displaced into the working classes, she can be fully condemned as sexually deviant.

The thrills of this thriller are thus intimately bound up with questions of female identity and guilt. The reader is mainly aligned with Blair, since he tells the story, and partakes of his power as representative of the Law to read appearances and finally to assign the feminine sexualities to their correct social positions. For this Betty Kane/Marion Sharpe reversal to be possible all kinds of unlikely textual rabbits have to be pulled out of hats: Betty Kane is found, for example, to have a photographic memory. And yet such manipulations point to the strength of the initial disturbance, the fear which runs through the text and which is never finally quelled – the fear precisely that female desire, the demands of feminine sexuality, can never be fully regulated through the definitions and limitations of class.

For this fear to be the centre of the text and its propelling force – the narrational impulse, if you like – is common enough but it takes on its own distinct and resonant form in the immediate post-war period.[9] For what is being asked through the question of feminine sexuality is both national and historical in their broadest senses. Before we even meet the Sharpes and their dilemma a 'condition of England' question has already been posed by Blair in the opening scene of the novel. The novel begins with the exploration of *his* doubts as to the pleasures and possibilities of being a middle class citizen after the war. The process whereby Betty Kane becomes a kind of psychic 'dumping ground' for all the fears originally inspired by Marion Sharpe is, therefore, a narrative strategy which works to relieve this initial 'trouble' and which thus functions as a dramatisation of the process of embourgeoisment itself – the psychic manoeuvres which accompany and allow economic change.

Set contemporaneously, *The Franchise Affair*[10] might perhaps be written off as simply the kind of popular fiction which is clearly right-wing in its explicit political commentary: through Blair, the way of life and the values of the English middle classes are constantly praised. But it is a social order whose ideal moment is seen to be *before* the war and it is from a sense of its fragility and fragmentation that the novel starts. In his office at Blair, Hayward and Bennett, Blair eulogises the small provincial town in which he has grown up and long wanted to take his designated place as country solicitor and worthy citizen. Milford, we are told, 'typified the goodness of life in England for the last three-hundred years' (p.8), its countryside 'quiet and confident and unchanged since the wars of the Roses' (p.13). This remarkable landscape is, of course, a profoundly middle class site (sight), a *tabula rasa* wiped clean of the chequered history of rural and urban struggles. Enemies to this mythological golden continuity are, not surprisingly, the local industrial town with its 'dirty red brick', proletarian holidays, cinemas, youths in pink shirts and the left intelligentsia whom Tey satirises in an invented publication, *The Watchman*. Far from being secure and immutable, all

the evidence points to this solid order being deeply
threatened and what is interesting is that Blair himself
expresses this ambivalence. He feels strangely restless,
unable to be content at the office with his Tuesday
digestives on the old lacquer tray. Marion Sharpe and
her problem come as a welcome disruption to routine;
her case is then both a threat to Milford and its ideal of
bourgeois respectability, and a desirable distraction from
it. The opening of the novel thus speaks to the fears
and desires of the post-war middle classes, to the
upheaval in social and sexual places the war had
caused, to the men and women who might be unable
to settle down after its excitement or who, worse still,
might not wish to.

Blair's journeys in search of evidence to vindicate the
Sharpes, through the landscapes of Midland town and
country, suburban growth and heavy industry, clearly
expresses the anxieties over social and economic
change through the issues of moral and sexual
regulation: what sort of social order, it asks, can
emerge from the wasteland of the Blitz when it turns
out to produce creatures like Betty Kane? The text
takes the form of a loaded question where the attempt
to reassert the importance of being bourgeois is
expressed through an interrogation of what constitutes
'normal' and desirable female sexuality. Feminine
sexuality is then the place where the discourses of class
difference can be consolidated and those of middle class
nationalism ultimately reaffirmed. Yet this is a far from
uncomplicated trajectory of identification for the
woman reader, and is achieved only at severe cost. For
if conventional middle class femininity is in the end
offered as the safest and most acceptable option, it is
noticeable by its actual absence in the text. In fact our
sympathies are directed towards those femininities
which exist on the margins, and whilst the girl ends up
punished for her sexual desires, Marion Sharpe is left

without *any* social or sexual place. In a sense the fiction tries to offer the reader the chance to have her cake and eat it: to endorse bourgeois norms in theory whilst actually enjoying the pleasure of their disruption. The risk is, I want to argue, a certain kind of textual indigestion.

Marion Sharpe and her mother are at first presented as social oddities, living alone in genteel poverty, products themselves more of the horse-breeding landed classes than of the Midlands bourgeoisie. Marion, as a type of upper middle class woman, is acceptably outside of the middle class norms, since her figure combines an appeal to the older and more desirable class status of Empire and aristocracy-fallen-on-hard-times which the middle classes have long both aped and despised. She is a bad housekeeper and a feeble cook, bored with domestic chores and fiercely independent, virginal without being sexless (her name suggests both her maidenliness and her acerbity). Indeed to Blair it is this very autonomy, the fact that she is so unlike his middle class girlfriends, that makes her sexually attractive – with her 'gipsy face' and bad manners. Marion is set against Blair's Aunt Lin in one of the many narrative pairings of different femininities. Aunt Lin is a mother figure, the type of conforming housewife, always running after Blair with an ashtray, dispensing solid English meals and endlessly polishing the hall table. Whilst she appears the only trustworthy middle class woman in the novel, she is nevertheless gently mocked throughout. Marion and her mother, outside the nuclear family, are not, however, simply appealing through their difference; living without men and amidst dire shortages was an experience shared by many women in 1948, and fresh in the minds of all.

Betty Kane, on the other hand, is the English schoolgirl *par excellence*, it seems – 'an ordinary sort of girl, after all – not the sort you would notice in a croc' (p.27), an allusion which nicely places her as both anonymous *and* middle class. An adopted child living in a decent suburban home, she is always seen from the outside. The narrative gives us a series of pictures of her, often literally in the form of newspaper photos, from which we must try to read off or interpret the sexuality from her candid young face. At this stage the reader, like Blair, is poised between the women, wondering whether Marion Sharpe's actions have been an understandable though pathological attempt on the part of a sex-starved spinster to solve the servant problem. Yet this appearance of innocence presents no difficulties to the Sharpes. When she is first confronted with Betty Kane, whom she swears she has never seen before, Marion's mother immediately asks, 'is the girl a virgin?'; Marion herself comments that Betty is obviously over-sexed (a pseudo-scientific way of imposing norms) because of the colour of her eyes ('faded navy blue', if you're interested) – an 'intuitive' observation which Blair reluctantly backs up. Already the link is made whereby the only way in which the girl can have spent a month away from home returning bruised and dishevelled is willingly to have been with a man. This 'logical' suggestion together with Marion's own attractiveness sways Blair into taking on the case and sets up its conclusion in advance.

The terms of Betty Kane's process of defilement are worth restating in full for the brutal righteousness with which an 'explanation' of her behaviour is offered. The schoolgirl in her 'nun's clothing' and grey court shoes turns out to be the product of that new post-war entity, 'the broken home', and her mother a 'goodtime gal' out every night with officers, actually enjoying the war. This 'unnatural' natural mother stuffed Betty full of sweets by way of compensation for maternal deprivation before she was farmed out during the Blitz, and the mother herself was suitably destroyed in a bomb blast. The true villain of the piece, the source of all the text's troubles, is then Betty's bad mother, who has apparently passed on nymphomania in the blood, blood which is, crucially, working class. This mixture of popular psychology and eugenics is offered to explain why, at 15, Betty has spent a month with a travelling salesman whom she picked up in the bar of a railway hotel. A class-based inheritance has been ratified, a legacy of tainted and inadequate femininity handed down from mother to daughter which the Sharpes, now visible as good objects, can be seen to contradict.

I want to stress, though, the full depth and force of the anxiety which this 'answer', the combination of an autonomous female sexuality with a working class aetiology, both attempts to allay and, paradoxically, reveals. It can be felt in the relish with which all the characters speak of punishing Betty Kane from the opening pages of the novel onward. Marion Sharpe dreams of torturing her and maintains, 'It affords me intense satisfaction that someone beat her black and blue' (p.36). Blair himself describes his desire for her righteous exposure in terms of an unconsciously sexual fantasy: 'I'm going to undress her in public. . . . I'm going to strip her of every rage of pretence, in open court, so that everyone will see her for what she is' (p.172). This is one of the places where the text 'informs against itself' as it were.[11] For what is going on is a complicated process of displacements which offer the reader symbolic pleasures. In effect the narrative now finally endorses the crime which it began by condemning. The beating of a 15-year-old girl into servile submission was the action originally seen as 'sick'. This degradation is now permissible in *fact* as well as in fantasy, once her low class position has been revealed. Yet the excessive and fixating language which Betty Kane provokes shows her to be the object of desire as well as of fear – the characters 'give themselves away'. For if Tey's solution to the enigmas of the text is superficially acceptable (Betty Kane is a bad working class girl, Marion Sharpe a good bourgeois), the language and the mechanisms of the plot reveal the ways in which bourgeois ideology must always over-compensate for its obsessional anxieties and the brutal repressiveness with which it must react to any threat to its terms. The really 'sick' twist to the tale comes in court when we discover that, far from being beaten by her male lover, Betty was punished by his wife. The story thus allows the pleasure of Betty's punishment to be performed without middle class guilt; the middle classes, it seems, can even get their dirty work done for them.

By the end of the novel, then, Betty Kane has become a kind of reservoir into which all the fears and desires of middle class, middle-aged heterosexuality have been poured. And yet the anxiety which is unleashed by her attempt to dislodging the anchors of class, sexuality and age (which ought to tie her to her social place) is never fully assuaged. For the process by which she is shown to be 'seething with unnameable emotions' (p.242) is necessarily based on an under-mining of middle class 'appearance', an erosion of its trustworthiness and confidence. If, as the narrative finally would have us believe, all's well because she wasn't *really* a nice middle class schoolgirl after all, how are we to be sure of what lurks beneath the innocent exteriors of all those other gym-slipped adolescents? On the other hand, too, there is still a problem with Marion Sharpe. Despite the clues which have been accumulated in favour of her social accept-ability (family connections with Blair's closest friend, Good Sherry and Sunday Lunches), Marion Sharpe was originally posed as a *critique* of middle class norms; this made us identify with her in the first place and distrust Betty Kane. She cannot, therefore, be fully recuperated or reincorporated back into Milford society without great damage being done to the plausibility, the 'realism' of the novel.

The climax of the novel is surprisingly but logically, then, not the trial of Betty Kane (which is a foregone conclusion) but the burning of the Sharpes' house, the Franchise, on the night of the trial. The house has also undergone subtle transofrmations in the course of the narrative; from being a slightly sinister, almost Gothic mansion (with its guilty secret in the attic), it has come to represent all that was good and uncomplicated about the 'old England' of the Empire's rulers and servants, of an upper middle class whose days, by 1948, are patently numbered.

'The Franchise is always the same. It has no frills' (p.223). Its destruction (by gangs of 'rural hooligans') is a necessary act for both the narrative and the middle class reader; it is a recognition of social change (at least to the extent of acknowledging the dominance of the middle middle classes with their 'foreign help' and less extravagant ways), and a sad farewell to an alternative which is still perceived as in many ways more attractive than its stolid successor.[12] Most importantly it leaves the Sharpes, the good mother and daughter, free-floating and displaced. Since it would not be plausible for Marion or her mother to become Milford housewives, what is Tey to do with the romantic possibility of a union between Blair and Marion which has been part of the 'interest' all along? Their marriage would be the ideal 'closure' and yet it presents very real structural problems for Tey since the attraction depends on Marion's 'difference'. Thus when, as the reader expects, Blair proposes, Marion replies 'in character', in a speech of admirable clear-sightedness, 'I am *not* a marrying woman. I don't want to put up with someone else's crochets, someone else's demands. . . . Mother and I suit each other perfectly because we make no demands on each other. . . . But no husband would do that' (p.251). When Blair objects to her life being lonely and empty, her retort is the nearest one comes to an outright rejection of the bourgeois ideal of the joys of motherhood and wifedom: 'A "full" life in my experience is usually full only of other people's demands.' Laying aside her golf club (and the 'piece of gutta-percha' she knocks around), she calmly announces her intention to take her mother to Canada.

Heresy indeed, and surely an appealing fantasy moment for any middle class woman reader. And yet is it not deeply suspect as a proto-feminist manifesto? For amongst the demands which a husband would make are presumably sexual ones. There is no possibility offered of Marion finding any sexual pleasure in her future life and her autonomy is bought at the price of sexual experience and desire, her protest against marriage and domesticity at the cost of her sexual needs. This is an attractive but profoundly disabling myth of independence – one which leaves out female sexual desire – and one which has been offered women in many guises. The *alter ego* of the housewife, soon to become the popular image of the 1950s – the 'Career Woman' – likewise guarantees the 'full life' of the wife and mother even as she claims the sterile independence of her own. Both images complement each other but actually work to secure femininity within the well-regulated choice between economic independence and sexual autonomy: no 'respectable' woman can have both. Marion's refusal is thus a kind of Pyrrhic victory, one which is quite in line with a femininity founded on duty and self-sacrifice. What narratives like this allow the reader to do is to displace those desires on to other women, bad objects, the working classes (or women of other races) for example. Against Marion Sharpe are set other inadequate options: Aunt Lin, domesticated and sexless, calling only for recipes and religion, and the rampant and deviant sexuality of proletarian girls deprived of good mothering. Finally it is she who tries to have it all, Betty Kane's adoptive mother, middle class, intelligent *and* pretty, who suffers most of all; she is made a fool of by her daughter and 'crucified' in court. Only the odd couple, the Sharpes, can be taken as any kind of model for female relations and they too are left ultimately 'disenfranchised'.

The ending too is left unsettled. In a last ditch attempt at a resolution Tey gives us a final page, tacked on almost, like an afterthought, in which the still restless Blair follows Marion on to the plane to Canada. We are not given wedding bells, however, but an ambiguous final attack on Blair's smugness; the plot is left hanging, literally, as well as symbolically, in mid-air. The reader cannot be given any satisfaction without textual of psychological disruption to the 'truth' which the narrative has set up. What it does in fact reveal is a truth of another sort: the 'true romance' (where the woman also has her desire), if it is to be possible at all, can only occur outside the bounds of middle class England and the social and sexual spaces it maps out for women, outside of its territories and narratives.

I would argue then that the novel cannot simply be read 'realistically', as describing the actual social options open to women – that is, if you dare to be different you'll end up in Canada – though emigration has long been a favoured solution to the problem of superfluous or undesirable elements of the population. Rather the text needs to be read as a pleasurable and contradictory fantasy, one in which the spread of femininities is both dictated and disrupted by the demands of class. Tey's text is not in this sense particularly special or unusual in reproducing the dilemmas of femininities regulated but never finally fixed by the prescriptions of class difference – such tensions have organised the novel since it was first written – but the specific ways in which such dilemmas and prescriptions are both imagined and expressed in the immediate post-war period *are* unique. Tey's text *is*, perhaps, unusual in that its contradictions are more manifest, its ending untypically 'open'. And yet the contradictions in the text which produce this lack of closure are themselves representative: the location of female sexual desire is a kind of vanishing point into which every other consensual or cohesive ideology threatens to disappear, including the realist form of the novel itself.

To find a way into the contradictions of women's lives in the period, it seems to me that a feminist must read such texts *symptomatically*, as speaking to us simultaneously of a resistance to, and a containment within, a normative bourgeois femininity. As Juliet Mitchell has recently suggested, we might find it helpful to think of women's writing, and more precisely the bourgeois novel, as the 'discourse of the hysteric', where 'normal' femininity is taken to be a profoundly social disease.[13] To see the woman writer as hysteric is more useful than seeing her as some essentialised female voice outside of history or the social, since it recognises our oppression within masculine discourse together with our ever-present resistance to it. Nor should we then be afraid of the novel as a bourgeois tradition since it is exactly *as* a bourgeois tradition that it comes to shape the history and to construct the dominant terms of what we continue to understand by 'woman'. As feminist literary critics and historians, we might begin to chart a kind of 'psychohistory' (or rather histories), a theorising of the formation of different subjectivities within different texts at different times, and for different purposes and pleasures. To read the more so-called 'highbrow' fiction of the period – the work of 'realists' like Barbara Pym, Elizabeth Taylor or Antonia White – need not then be wholly divorced from a feminist reading of the vast numbers of thrillers, romantic and historical novels which women wrote and read. They all offer their women readers symbolic landscapes of lost and found identities, of simultaneous rebellion and submission, an exploration of social constraints and often a deeply pleasurable resolution of them which is – often impossibly – both individually and fully social. How else is one to begin to historicise a text like Barbara Comyns's *The Vet's Daughter*, written in 1959 but set in the late nineteenth century, the autobiography of Alice Rowlands, an oppressed lower middle class girl who learns to levitate and eventually, at the novel's climax, ascends into the heavens from Clapham Common? Comyns has perhaps displaced her discussion of contemporary femininity back to earlier moments of the formation of its bourgeois terms, in order to give her reader a fantastic escape from its bounds; the novel is a disappearing trick, a wish fulfilment and yet also, finally, a self-effacement since its success demands Alice's death.

Feminism has long argued that the conditions of our psychic and our material lives determine and express each other, and that both must needs be changed. To make connections between those lives and the variety of written fictions women and men produce, to try to relate the pleasures and expectations of reading and writing to the patterns and structures of life within a patriarchal capitalist society, remains a crucial and fully historical part of feminism's project: in reading how those lives have been endlessly re-imagined we try to underline the terms for our own continued change.

This is what it means to map out a common culture which we call 'women's writing'. If we see women's writing as a history, then such texts show woman to be a subject-in-process, always becoming, and the connections we choose to make between 'women' and 'writing' are enormously, and centrally, political. Even if we read the 1950s as one of the bleakest times for women, women's writing reminds us of our productive energy in the face of passivity, our demands for pleasure despite 'duty'. In revealing the fictions which keep us sane and active on all levels of our linguistic existence, a feminist attention to women's writing is part of feminism's desire to achieve a more compassionate and generous understanding of human consciousness and its effects, of how political changes come about, of what we choose to call history, and of the extent to which the resistance of all peoples, their capacity to *represent* themselves, is always possible. For if, to adapt Marx, we need to believe, as feminists, that all women can make history as well as be made by it, then the making of representations is perhaps the most uniquely human activity – the activity by which we live. Literature, then, as a site of our most self-conscious articulations, might help us to see how it is that we can enter into ideologies of the most oppressive kinds – in Mitchell's phrase, 'to live ideas' – whilst never being fully subsumed or positioned by them. Thus for us in the 1980s, writing the history of women and their writing is still one of our most pleasurable and inspiring *and* political projects, engaging as it must with the fictions which make us women, as well as the fictions we make.

Notes

1 See, for example, V. Bogdanor and R. Skidelsky (eds), *The Age of Affluence 1951–1964*, London, Macmillan, 1970; A. Marwick,

British Society Since 1945, Harmondsworth, Penguin, 1982; J. Ryder and H. Silver, Modern English Society, London, Methuen, 1970.

2 A word coined in the early 1950s to express the continuity of policy between the outgoing Labour Chancellor of the Exchequer, Hugh Gaitskell, and the incoming Conservative one, R. A. Butler.

3 See D. Riley, War In the Nursery, London, Virago, 1983; J. Weeks, Sex, Politics and Society, Harlow, Longman, 1981; E. Wilson, Only Halfway To Paradise – Women in Post-War Britain: 1945–1968, London, Tavistock, 1980.

4 See, for example, the discussion of the shifting values of 'the Movement's' poetry in B. Morrison, The Movement: English Poetry and Fiction of the 1950s, Oxford, Oxford University Press, 1980.

5 For one recent account of the period which does attend to the question of sexual difference, see J. Dollimore's excellent chapter 'The challenge of sexuality' in A. Sinfield (ed.), Society and Literature 1945–1970, London, Methuen, 1983.

6 These arguments are also taken up by S. Alexander in 'Women, class and sexual differences in the 1830s and 1840s: some reflections on the writing of a feminist history', History Workshop Journal, no.17, Spring 1984, and by J. Mitchell in Women: The Longest Revolution, London, Virago, 1984.

7 See Mitchell, op.cit., pp. 242–5 for a discussion of the psychoanalytic definition of fantasy – 'an imaginary scene in which the subject is the protagonist and in which, in distorted manner, a wish is fulfilled. Phantasy is the setting for the desire (wish) which came into being with its prohibition (absence of object)' (p. 242).

8 For further discussion of this point see T. Lovell, 'Writing like a woman: a question of politics', in F. Barker et al. (eds), The Politics of Theory, Essex, University of Essex, 1983.

9 T. Modleski, Loving With A Vengeance: Massproduced Fantasies for Women, London, Methuen, 1984, brilliantly explores the textual and sexual politics of romance fiction and television soap operas, raising similar questions about the power of fantasy in writing and reading.

10 All page references are to The Franchise Affair by Josephine Tey, Harmondsworth, Penguin, 1951 (first published London, Peter Davies, 1948).

11 Some of the terms of my analysis have been derived from the work of the Marxist literary theorist Pierre Macherey, and in particular from *A Theory of Literary Production*, London, Routledge & Kegan Paul, 1978. Macherey's work is usefully discussed in Modleski, op. cit., pp. 110–14.

12 There are similar tensions and contradictions in much 'country house' literature of the period. See, for example, my own analysis of Daphne du Maurier's *Rebecca*, 'Returning to Manderley: romance fiction, female sexuality and class', *Feminist Review*, no.16, 1984.

13 Mitchell, op. cit., p. 289.

From the BBC television serialisation of *Penmarric*, 1979

8
Family romances: the contemporary popular family saga

CHRISTINE BRIDGWOOD

Realism and romance

It has often been pointed out that in contemporary popular romantic novels the external world drops away from the text except as a setting, leaving the hero and heroine viewing each other in a one-dimensional universe.[1] If one function of romance is to move woman from her position of heterosexual subordination to one of unified and secure subjectivity, then the romantic relationship is the place where women find their authentic selves and have their identities established, completed and confirmed – in a kind of natural, absolute possession outside of any social, economic, or political context. The narrative leads to resolution through heterosexual union, which closes down the possibility of other desires and other narratives, and relegates women to a position beyond culture and history, firmly placed in the realm of 'nature' and 'eternal truth'.

In the family saga, however, marriage, with its consequent integration into the social order, is never the straightforward means of precipitating the narrative's climax and conclusion that it is in romance. The saga differs from other popular fiction genres in its lack of drive towards narrative closure and in its tendency to begin at the point where romance stops. The romantic fiction is structured into a coherent linear

167

narrative around a few moments of transcendence (the first glimpse of the hero, the first sign of his admiration in the gaze, the kiss), whereas the family saga is, by definition, structured as a long-term process.

This brings me to the relationship of the family saga to realism.[2] Although many of the saga's strategies remain those of classic realism, the form does lack some of the most important conventions of dominant ways of storytelling – the impetus towards the resolution of the plot, the circularity of a narrative that solves all problems it encounters, the successful completion of the individual's quest and, to some extent, the process of identification. Any full identification between reader and character (which has been seen as another of the principal means by which the realist text secures the recognition of its particular representations as 'real', diverting the reader from what is contradictory in the text to what s/he already 'knows'), tends to be undermined in the saga narrative. Here, three-dimensionality of character is subordinated to the structure of repetition, contrast, variation and antithesis by which the text constructs its cross-generational profile of the *family* in its multiformity. In this sense individual characters in the saga are merely facets of a collective character constructed at a broader narrative level. The conflicts and problems which propel the saga forward tend to be structured in a series of oppositions, and it is the function of many of the characters to carry one or other of the terms of the opposition, as in the antithetical pairs of rebel/conformist, good mother/bad mother, promiscuous/faithful, rightful heir/rival claimant. In discussing the texts I will be considering how far this undermining of any full process of identification and the lack of drive towards narrative closure combine with other features to interrogate such primary ideological agencies as the family, romantic love and nationalism.

Writing and reading

As a genre, the popular family saga is remarkable for employing a marketing strategy which appears to be attempting to reduce the sense of distance and difference between writers and readers. Most begin with a detailed potted author's biography presenting writer to reader:

> 'Danielle started working for *Supergirls* . . . when the recession hit, the firm went out of business and Danielle "retired" to write her first book, *Going Home*. She moved to California, seeking "an easier climate, gentler people and a better place to write".'[3]

> 'Susan Howatch . . . was an only child and her father was killed in the Second World War . . . after working for a year as an articled clerk she was bored with practical law and decided to devote herself to writing. . . . '[4]

> 'Catherine Gaskin married an American and settled down in New York for ten years. . . . '[5]

Apart from the marked contrast to the anonymity and interchangeability of, say, Mills & Boon authors, what is striking about these doubtless carefully selected biographical details is the implication that the author, despite her glamour, is really not so different from the reader herself – she too has experienced common disasters (the firm went out of business, her father died), dilemmas (she was bored) and delights (she married and settled down). Cosy, intimate, first-name terms are being established.

Furthermore, the process of writing, although documented as being arduous and time-consuming –

'She began *The Thorn Birds*, writing it at night, after her work as head technician in a neurophysiology laboratory had ended. . . . '[6]

'Writing this book has been rather like writing a real-life detective story, with the facts given in old letters, stories and newspaper cuttings forming the framework around which my tale is woven.'[7]

– is still depicted as springing almost spontaneously from the author's own history and experience. Judith Saxton, for example, dedicated *The Pride* (1981) to her grandmother and stresses in her acknowledgments that the idea for the book 'sprang from my grandmother's charmingly written memoirs'.[8] This appeal to the unmediated matrix of (specifically female) experience, memory and writing as spontaneous growth, is of course belied by the complexity of the actual texts, but the ideology of the text as sold to the reader is that of oral history: we have all, as women, got such stories to tell, and, given the necessary effort, perhaps could. Look, for example, at the following extracts from the author biographies prefacing each saga:

'Her northern roots are strongly reflected in her work. She is an author who sets her charaters against a backcloth she knows well.'[9]

'The desire to write, she says, has been her one and only lifeline during a tumultuous and changeable life.'[10]

'Her work with "wayward" girls and her own family has increased her interest in the female situation, present and past.'[11]

The implication is that anyone could have a go, as it is too in a *Guardian* interview with Colleen McCullough (15 April 1977) which stresses her rise from ordinary student nurse to world-famous novelist.

In this sense, the marketing of the family saga produces significantly different implications from the escapism generally attributed to romance. The ideology of authorship in saga publicity appears to be directing the reader back into the potentialities of her own experience, into her family history as potential saga, to writing as a 'natural' product of living, achievable through application, strength of will, a harnessing of the general capabilities that women display in their everyday domestic and work situations. This universalisation of the potential power to write such fiction is matched by a universalisation of the fiction's material – despite the variants of geographical, historical and class settings, the saga families' fictionalised lives are nevertheless structured around a number of dilemmas which can be essentially similar for women of entirely different national, social and economic groups.

The construction of the family as a universal form, then, produces a series of crucial mediations between writer and reader, writing and reading, the production of a text and the pre-text of 'experience'. Linked through the shared experience of the family, the writer is merely a reader who has got her act together. Reading can be a rehearsal for your own transition to writing, and experience, through the family's historical dimension, is already on the way to becoming text. Far from being positioned in a simply passive, powerless relation to the text, the reader of the saga, in order for the text's central terms of family and experience to function, is established in a curious space of creative potentiality; poised between her personal experience, which is being valorised as potential 'material', and a writing which declares itself as the 'material-ised' experience of someone not unlike herself. For sagas to work the reader must be, at least potentially, the next bestseller herself.

The family

The great subject of the novelist, as Stephen Heath has suggested,[12] has been crucially the family – the family as bridge between the individual and society, the private and the public. It has been posited as the site of the conflict and resolution of these terms in the world apart which it purports to offer: marriage and the family, a firm social unit offering a privileged mode of individuality and a haven of personal happiness. In this sense, the modern family saga explores the same terrain as the realist novel of the ninetenth century: the family and its dynastic considerations such as inheritance, the continuation of the male line, family duty, and alliances with outsiders and rivals. In the nineteenth century novel what is often at stake is the integration of a male pattern of inherited social power. Novels such as *Pride and Prejudice*, *Middlemarch* and *Daniel Deronda*, which are concerned with the specifically *female* relation to this system of social power, have tended to represent women settling within that system through a struggle towards marriage, which once again occupies a decisive position in the 'individual and society' organization, proposed as a mediation between the two.

Where the contemporary popular saga differs, as it differs too from popular romance, is in its exploration not of the achievement of that state but of the maintenance of it. Although the saga undoubtedly works, on one level, to reinforce prevailing ideological definitions of the family, in other ways it challenges the concept of the family as definable purely in terms of blood relations and kinship, and moves towards a redefinition of the meanings of the primacy and exclusivity of the family.[13] The 'family' in Catherine Gaskin's *Family Affairs*, for example, consists of an all-female group of two sisters, a woman who was briefly married to their father, her stepdaughter and a friend, all living in a house split into separate flats.

It is partly this redefinition and extension of the family in the saga that allows its representation as a highly sexualised site, a representation which (apart from guaranteeing a good read!) resists western industrial society's conceptualisation of the family as at once legitimating and concealing sexuality. The question of what actually constitutes the family is repeatedly stretched and renegotiated in the saga, activating conflicting discourses which are not easily contained by the text. Ideological contradictions within the family are opened up and then an attempt is made to sidestep them by by the imaginary resolution of the redefined, expanded and sexualised family.

The Thorn Birds: historical process and common sense

An issue which continually resurfaces when thinking about the popular family saga is that of the contradictory effects of the narrative's extended time-span, with its invocation of historical process. Lillian S. Robinson, in her discussion of historical romance,[14] argues that this kind of text obliges the reader to entertain *some* definition of history. By her account, the family saga, in its representation of history and women's lives over time, would necessarily show to some extent the overlapping and contradictory ways in which sexual differences are instituted under different conditions at different historical moments, with the sense of historical process working to interrogate existing power relations and ideological definitions of sexuality and the social. And yet, as this analysis of *The Thorn Birds* attempts to show, it is precisely this historical materiality and the extended temporal perspective of the family saga which serves to make the social and sexual order appear as the natural state of things.

The Thorn Birds (1977) chronicles three generations of the Cleary family and their relation to the family home, Drogheda, a sheep farm in southern Australia. The narrative follows, in social terms, the advance from the slavery of frontier womanhood to the emancipation of the modern woman on near equal terms in a man's world. The Clearys are a non-dynastic dynastic family, the third generation consisting only of one daughter, Justine. Her grandmother Fee had eight sons (girls didn't count), and her mother two children, but Justine is able to repudiate the whole breeding business – 'Not bloody likely! Spend my life wiping snotty noses and cacky bums?'[15] Femininity is placed in the text as a site of social change and it is made clear that the pull of the homeland must be resisted to achieve this change. A critical point occurs at the end of the narrative when Justine has to choose whether to return home to Drogheda or to continue her career in Europe. She is on the point of flying back to Australia ('I want something safe, permanent, enduring, so I'm coming home to Drogheda, which is all those things'[16]), marrying a local boy and retracing her roots after her European flutter, but is stopped in the end by the letter from her mother advising her to stay away for the sake of her career and happiness. Justine in the penultimate climactic scene is shown rejecting Drogheda and the bondage it represents to her.

Superficially, then, the moral trajectory of *The Thorn Birds* is towards the acceptance of a necessary distancing from tradition, the land, the home, one's country (all signified by the property Drogheda) in order to create space for individual growth. The bonds of the family are denied (Drogheda can give Justine nothing), yet at the same time sanctified (it takes her grandmother and mother, blood relations, to know her well enough to realise that Drogheda can give her nothing). What is more, Justine is able to move decisively outside the family circle only by moving into another stable, approved societal unit – that of marriage.

This last point suggests another discourse at work in the text alongside that of women's 'emancipation', and which undercuts and problematises it. This is the discourse of common sense – 'that's life' – the stoic acceptance of fate. The text is threaded through with the lugubrious insights of now enlightened characters – 'we can't change what we are . . . we are what we are, that's all . . . what must be, must be . . . it is the way things are . . . it's just common sense.'[17] This discourse produces the idea of a human essence which exists independently of the social, bringing with it the category of an essential femininity.

The appeal in the text to fate, common sense and an essentially masochistic female 'nature' are all synthesised in the legend of the thorn bird which prefaces and completes the text and is invoked at one crucial moment in the narrative. The thorn bird, following 'an immutable law',[18] spends its life searching for a thorn tree and having found it 'impales itself on the longest, sharpest spine'[19] and dying sings 'one superlative song, existence the price'.[20] The suggestion of feminine masochistic surrender to the victimising phallus is transparent, and is made explicit in Meggie's final-page reverie when, in epitomising her life-long frustrated love for Ralph, she reflects, 'I did it all myself. I have no one else to blame'.[21] The final words of the text reach out to implicate its readers in this masochism:

> The bird with the thorn in its breast . . . is driven by it knows not what to impale itself and die singing. At the very instant the thorn enters there is no awareness in it of the dying to come . . . but we, when we put the thorns in our breasts, we know. We understand. And still we do it. Still we do it.[22]

In Meggie and Ralph's retrospective discussion of their relationship, the legend is invoked by Meggie to exonerate Ralph for his sacrifice of her to his clerical ambitions. For Ralph, the 'thorn' can be that of ambition, the will to power, but for women it is necessarily that of love and sexual experience. Female subjectivity is constructed within sexual categories, and even the shift from this with the third generation makes it clear that the thorn is only slightly less sharp for the autonomous, career-oriented modern woman.

There is then a contradiction in *The Thorn Birds* between the opening out with the third generation to a more independent, self-determining lifestyle for women (albeit within marriage) and the undercutting of any idea of social change by the discourse of fate and cyclical repetition which frames the text and operates powerfully within it – a contradiction which is clearly played out in the final few paragraphs of the text, which consists of an evocation of 'the same endless, unceasing cycle'[23] and yet simultaneously asserts that it is 'time for Drogheda to stop'[24] in order for progress and change to be made possible. This contradiction is common to most popular family sagas and can be explained further by reference to the double temporal structure which they are based on.

The saga is structured upon two parallel temporal axes, the one short, the other extended. The shorter axis produces a dramatic structure of various episodes, incidents and climaxes which revolve around and are supported by concepts of progress, the individual and (given that the text foregrounds female experience) the feminine – in *The Thorn Birds*, the life histories of Fee, Meggie and Justine. The extended axis, however, works to defuse this structure of individual drama, experience and change by overlaying it with a discourse of the 'long view' which speaks in favour of tradition, the family, the heritage, the dynasty. This is the ironic overview at work in *The Thorn Birds'* evocation of destiny, common sense and time as healer. The text itself has an investment in this ironic overview – it is after all on this axis that its key terms of family and saga are situated.

The tensions I have pointed to in *The Thorn Birds* stem not merely from the long–term/short–term antithesis, but also from the contradictions inherent in this ironic position itself. For irony, while declaring itself as an analytical, 'deconstructive' mode, is also classically conservative in its operations. It implies that if a long enough view is taken, all current events and individual dramas are insignificant in the face of the immensity of life ('the rhythmic endless cycle'[25]). But individual histories can be swallowed up and individual experience ironised only because the longer time-span they are being set against is itself subjected to no questioning. The text rests on an unchallenged basis of tradition, history and family continuity, and in the end takes up a position entirely identified with these concepts, although of course some interplay between the two temporal perspectives is necessary for the narrative to function.

This then is the structural contradiction at work in the family saga. What *The Thorn Birds* in particular makes clear is that the ironic, male, long-term overview which is ostensibly in conflict with the specifically female short-term perspective does in fact hold some positive uses for women. The ironic 'life's like that' philosophy becomes a way of validating the suffering and frustration that Fee and Meggie's lives bring them. This is acted out in a great number of small details and incidents throughout the text, particularly in the scenes depicting their later relationship as two ageing women. Meggie as a girl was ignored by Fee precisely because of her femaleness, and the development traced in the narrative of their relationship, culminating in Fee's admission that 'I used to think having a daughter wasn't nearly as important as having sons, but I was wrong . . . a daughter's an equal'[26] constitutes a powerful representation of female bonding. Like Justine's life story, it would seem to gesture towards an ideal of progress, towards social change making personal change possible. Yet this representation is critically undermined by the discourses which I've shown as clustering around the extended, ironic temporal axis; nothing really changes, everything comes full circle, 'history does repeat itself'.[27] Meggie and Fee are constructed as women bound together by the inexorable patterns and cycles of nature, fate, family and love, agreeing, when looking back over their lives, that 'memories are a comfort, once the pain dies down'.[28]

The mother–daughter relationship echoes the rest of the text by interrogating female subject positions in the framework of short-term drama and incident, while in the same breath recuperating any disturbance by setting it in the safer context of the 'long view'. This is how history in the saga works as a double-edged discourse; it is at once the sharp nudge of awareness of historical process – the 'vision of historical possibility'[29] discussed by Lillian S. Robinson – and the soothing balm of an ideology of stoical acceptance which naturalises the social and sexual status quo, and is ultimately dependent upon essentialist categories of femininity.

Penmarric: female subjectivity and class identity

'I was ten years old when I first saw the inheritance
and twenty years old when I first saw Janna Roslyn,
but my reaction to both was identical. I wanted
them.'[30]

The opening lines of *Penmarric* (1971) firmly establish
the text's central terms. Immediately, women and
property are signified together, encompassed by the
male gaze as objects to be possessed, around which
male desire and patriarchal law are organised. Women
are defined in *Penmarric* as occupying a tangential
position in relation to production, culture and action –
unlike the majority of sagas, which foreground female
experience, it is the male line, male history, male
power relationships and male labour which structure
the text. What the privileging of the masculine in the
textual system does is make room for the dissection of
exactly how men construct women as a mythical
'other' against which man takes his definition, placing
her as a constitutive function in society rather than
among its active producers.

In *Penmarric*, as in many family sagas, the function of
historical distance is to clear a site for the representation
of class and sexual inequalities without being obliged
either to criticise or to defend them directly. It is
possible to form a set of political meanings around a
particular culture set elsewhere in place and time, while
using this historical and geographical dislocation
precisely as a means of defusing that declared political
consciousness. Once again, 'history' in the family saga
works in complex ways, as an imaginative space in
which both to represent social and political injustice,
and at the same time evade the implications of that
representation by an appeal to history itself: this is how

it was, we are not concerned with how it is now.

Within the cushioned space created by historical dislocation, the text presents a relentless analysis of how sexual relations are implicated with those of class. Gender identity is shown to be crucially informed by wider social relations and roles, and masculinity to be constituted through relations of power which work towards the ordering of sexuality and patriarchal right. The relation between female subjectivity and class identity is brutally exposed; class is defined through sexual difference, and vice versa. At no point, though, is the reader invited to make connections between then and now; it is precisely because of historical distancing that the text can summon up such an *exposé* while still securely endorsing the contemporary status quo.

Penmarric traces the history of a rich, landed Cornish family, the Castallacks, from 1890 to the end of the Second World War, beginning with the young Mark Castallack's desire for working-class Janna Roslyn. The three versions of femininity entertained by the text make it clear that sexuality is split across class lines. Specific forms of social control are exercised over women but Clarissa, through her wealth and social power, is able to subvert them while Janna, because of 'the lot of the lower classes and sundry other social circumstances',[31] is obliged to conform. Rose Parrish, however, as representative of the bourgeoisie, transgresses both class and sexual boundaries in her affair with the aristocratic Mark Castallack and the narrative has to restore her as good object to her rightful place within patriarchy – within familial relations.

This is transacted in the text through an opposition between Rose and Janna's class positions. Although Janna becomes Mark's wife, in offering her the fairy-tale motif of chivalrous rescue from penury, Mark also bears with him the ideological burden of that motif: that being raised from a dependent class position only intensifies Janna's awareness of class inadequacy. Her shift in class position, achieved solely through Mark's beneficence, is shown to be only precariously maintained, and to be wholly dependent upon the continuation of that beneficence. Despite elocution lessons to reduce her Cornish accent and reading to widen her vocabulary, 'that by now familiar burden of inadequacy'[32] haunts her, and the scene of her discovery of her husband's secret life with Rose Parrish is dramatised in class terms – 'She was a lady'[33] – and for Janna increases the risks of being 'imprisoned forever in solitary confinement behind those iron walls of class'.[34] When Mark tires of her, it is to class that he appeals for his justification: 'that was the whole tragedy, wasn't it, my dear, you never were a lady and you never could be'[35] a point which Janna only endorses – 'my voice grated Cornish in my ears.'[36]

From this point on in the text, Janna is not given a voice, and is represented solely through the second generation's narratives, which insist upon the necessity for her of shoring up her own precarious class identity by the disparagement of others. In Philip's narrative, for example, Janna is represented as desperately hanging on to the class position she so painfully achieved in her youth by an exercise in systematic self-deception which denies her own class origins.

Penmarric is structured around five autobiographical narratives which each cover a different period of time, presented by Mark, Janna, and three of the sons. The authenticity of each narrative is thrown into question by the next, as the reader is confronted by mutually modifying or contradictory versions of 'reality'. In offering several conflicting subject positions from which it can be read, the text undermines the consistency and continuity of the subject. For example, a disturbingly fractured, incoherent image of femininity is constructed by the representation of a single woman as seen from several viewpoints by different characters at different historical moments. The status of Janna in the text shifts as the reader sees her initially through the 20-year-old Mark's eyes as a mysterious, aloof, enigmatic object of desire, then through her own discourse as faltering and uncomfortable in the class position he has raised her to, then as mediated variously through the different versions of her offered up by the other narrative voices.

The implication that there exists no essential truth, and that the most that can be offered (as is done by each 'autobiography' while deludedly offering itself up as the truth) is different versions of reality, is crucially implicated with the concept of 'the long view' which underpins the text. With *The Thorn Birds*, I tried to show how the extended temporal axis, while working in favour of patriarchal ideology, offered women an essentially comforting and quietistic perspective, but in *Penmarric* the ironic, long-term perspective works in less palliative, more complex ways. Firstly, the process of ageing is shown to have culturally different meanings and consequences for women and for men, being positively valued in the case of men, and negatively in that of women, and this immediately problematises women's relationship to the 'long-view' perspective. Secondly, whereas in *The Thorn Birds* the extended perspective, endorsed by the thorn bird legend, encodes a 'wise' acceptance of women's suffering for love, in *Penmarric* it functions more as an analytical mode, particularly in relation to the question of love, as when Jan-Yves defends his engagement before his mother with 'We love each other!', and Janna replies, 'Is that a magic incantation to ward off evil? Love can die, Jan-Yves, and don't tell me it can't because it can. I know.'[37] Like most other family sagas, *Penmarric* effectively dismantles the romantic ideal of lifetime monogamous attachment. Janna, for example, realises that what she thought of as love for Laurence Castallack was in fact a question of convenience, and even when she attempts to shore up her sense of identity by remembering what she felt for Mark, she is left with lack and emptiness – 'I thought numbly: I did love him, I did – oh God, tell me that I loved him once! But God was silent.'[38]

The long view in *Penmarric* works to demystify that cornerstone of bourgeois morality, marriage for love, and marital happiness is shown not as a final state but as precarious in the face of time. The different versions of reality mediated by the various autobiographical narratives are thus underpinned and reinforced by those different versions constructed by, and across, time. Mark and Janna's marriage is represented not only through different narrative voices but also through an extended temporal perspective; what was experienced by Mark as a serious, indeed rhapsodic affair is remembered years later as a ludicrous childish infatuation.

In this uncertain, shifting environment, the text posits a permanent crisis of identity which must be resolved by remembering the history of the individual as subject: the 'autobiography' would seem to be the representation of identity as the coherence of a past safely negotiated and reappropriated, but this is then disrupted by the existence of not merely one account but five. In fictions where several different points of view operate, coherence is usually maintained by one point of view (often that of the omniscient narrator) establishing itself as dominant. The reader of *Penmarric*, however, is denied this dominant perspective and its provision of a secure place from which she or he can interpret the text. The final narrative, that of Jan-Yves, despite its potential for a 'summing up', does not function as the privileged discourse which sets all the others in place, but rather as the place where the very system of values which has supported the text (tradition, heritage, the family, the mores of the aristocracy) are seen to be eroded by social and political change.

Family Affairs: the paternal and the political.

I have tried to show that the family saga steers a course between using history and the family as a means of *exposing* the interrelated dynamics of gender, class and power, and attempting a *recuperation* of the disturbances caused by this exposure through an appeal to precisely those same concepts of history and family. With Catherine Gaskin's *Family Affairs* (1980), the stretch of the novel's time-span into the 1980s problematises any use of 'historical process' and 'the long view', creating difficulties for the text in carrying out this containment. These difficulties are exacerbated, too, by the evasion in *Family Affairs* of any outright foregrounding of class and gender issues (unlike in, for example, *Penmarric*) and the reaching towards an imaginary realm in which such conflicts might be transcended in a state of full and unproblematic female subjectivity. The novel follows the metamorphosis of Kelly from cook's daughter at the Australian sheep station Pentland into Lady Brandon, member of a powerful and famous English family. Kelly's first marriage to the glamorous son of the owner of Pentland and their move to England are the initial steps in this ascent.

Whereas *Penmarric* used Janna's radical shift in class position through marriage to represent the solidity of that class system which renders any such shift partial and problematic, particularly for women, Kelly's meteoric rise is rather an attempt to assert the unimportance of class. Yet Kelly's move from the obscurity of her class background to her public position as the wife of famous men cannot avoid showing how the personal, the supposedly private sphere, is traversed by forces which the text attempts to maintain are external to it, and as such is revealed to be a profoundly ideological construct. The sub-text which is generated by this tension is concerned with *how* Kelly has advanced her social and class position (i.e. through various sexual alliances given the name of love) and the consequent precariousness of her identity within that class position. For if Kelly has crossed 'the divide between the servants and the Family',[39] she has done so precisely to enact another kind of servitude as mother, sexual servicer, emotional healer and publicity aid.

The geographical shift from Australia to England allows a certain camouflaging of Kelly's inferior class status – she is 'an Australian' rather than any particular class, and often unconcernedly acknowledges her origins at significant moments. On the other hand, however, her geographical displacement works in tandem with her class alienation to make it difficult for her ever to 'place' herself securely, caught ambiguously between Australian and English identities, as she is between working-class and aristocratic status. This is registered in the precariousness of her position, the necessity of servitude to maintain that position, and a self which at moments seems to be predicated upon a central absence, a vague but pervasive sense of failure – 'She had no life beyond Greg's and Laura's needs. The vacuum was achingly there.'[40] Given this emptiness, it is hardly surprising that soon after Greg's death, Kelly is eager to 'grope her way towards a new identity as Charles Brandon's wife'.[41] Charles figures as the classic family saga man – powerful, yet nurturant, supportive and understanding.[42] The introduction of him as a Conservative MP initiates the text's overt involvement with politics. *Family Affairs* is never quite comfortable with Charles's conservatism, and from his first appearance hedges it round with qualifications – 'He was known as a thoroughgoing Conservative, but an independently-minded one.'[43] The authorial voice hastens to assure us of his liberal stance on Vietnam – 'For a Conservative he had taken a surprising line there. From the beginning he had been violently against America's involvement',[44] of his populism – 'There was something in him that appealed to the gut reaction of patriotism in his largely working-class voters',[45] and of his lack of wealth.

In fact the text is so anxious about Charles's politics that they are usually defused into a kind of personal moral code, matters of right and wrong which are above mere 'politics', and his actions are mitigated by an appeal to a kind of aristocratic patriotism which offers itself as a moral discourse rising above issues of class and gender. An evacuation of the political is carried out by the construction of a persistent personal/political antithesis which is resolved in favour of the personal. This is particularly clear in the text's handling of the political differences between Charles and his daughter Kate, ex-London School of Economics student, social worker, East End party-goer and Labour Party activist. When Charles stands as an MP, Kate campaigns in the same borough in support of the Labour candidate, but this, far from causing Kate to be cut off without a penny, is merely a matter of 'Tory blue and Labour red ribbons embracing in the middle of the High Street'[46] and 'much laughter over the dinner table'.[47] The strength of the family bond negates political differences to the extent that Kate's response to her father's winning the seat can be 'Isn't it wonderful that Father's back in the House again?'[48] It is here that the ironic, long-view perspective is brought in precisely to defuse the political, the implication being that in the face of that extended perspective and the strength and continuity of the family, politics is an ephemeral sphere; family members may twist and turn politically but they are still, in the end, family. Witness Kate's political turnaround: because her politics are structured, like her father's, by her personal moral code, making 'the word "love" shine from among the statistics',[49] she soon becomes 'restless under the strictures of her Party'[50] and, unsurprisingly enough, ends up standing as a Conservative (Independent, of course) in her father's old parliamentary seat, declaring, 'I'm not for Socialism for its own sake. I want this to be a just and equable and free society.'[51] Political retrenchment takes place in the name of both individualism and the place where the individual is shown to find her authentic definition, the family.

Charles's death instigates the formation of the unlikely household of unrelated women that constitutes the family for the main part of *Family Affairs*. It is a fantasy of a matriarchal household, each person living separately yet with a pool of support and companionship. This redefined family posits gender as neutralising class and racial difference (Russian Marya and working-class Mrs Cass also belong to it) and this is the place where Kelly feels most secure. The fantasy works to deconstruct the family as a natural unit and reconstruct it as a social one, particularly in Kate's decision to bring up a baby within the household rather than with a man. A woman friend is present at the birth and the baby is looked after by the whole household, while the anxious, redundant father hovers ineffectually in the background. Yet, paradoxically, the baby is able to have no 'family' precisely because he has the weight of 'The Family' supporting him – 'John Michael Brandon was baptised and received into the Church of England with all due ritual. He wore the christening robe the Brandons have worn for two hundred years. And no one will ever call him a bastard.'[52] This effectively depoliticises any understanding of Kate's decision to have a baby outside heterosexual partnership, while continuing her career, as being linked to her socialist politics, and places it safely in the realm of the personal as one of Kate's endearing eccentricities. A disconcerting slippage is apparent through this episode: Kate keeps her surname and the baby is to take it, yet she assumes that only if the baby is a boy will the family name be continued – if it is a girl she'll marry and take her husband's name. This reversion to the most conventional sexual/familial ideology reveals how far her sexual radicalism is operable only within the closed, mythical space of the matriarchal household.

This female family offers Kelly a haven from the strain of maintaining her precariously achieved social position, although her security is persistently undermined by the presence of the Pages. Their position as housekeepers, their careful discarding of their accents, their striving to achieve middle-class status and their ambiguous relationship to the Brandon family are recognised by Kelly as threatening echoes of her own past efforts. Anglo-Indian Chris Page and his mother are outsiders in both class and racial terms, but this situates them at the centre of *Family Affairs'* discourse on national and cultural difference, marking out a site where 'foreignness' and 'mixedness' are encoded as transgressive and corrupting. This circulation of racial and cultural otherness finally explodes in the exposure of Chris as blackmailer and betrayer, necessitating his murder if a 'healthy' social order is to be maintained. But in defying the patterns established for social interaction by the text, this blast of 'abnormal', monstrous behaviour which (dis-)organises the last section of the text hints at a series of radical and irresolvable contradictions buried deep within both the system of the text and the total system of economic and social interactions which constitutes its

known world. More surprising even than the exposure
of Nick's financial double-dealings is Chris Page's
disclosure of himself as Charles's illegitimate son, and
of Charles himself (now long dead) as a Russian spy,
the Fourth Man in the Burgess, Maclean and Philby
affair: sexual and political betrayal are signified together, both involving a mingling with the other, the
foreign. Chris Page exposes the dirty cellarage of the
text, the hidden reality by which the Brandon dynasty
exists, but by allocating this task to a character who has
already been branded as sly and untrustworthy, and then
killing him off, the text neatly avoids having to finally
indicate the exact truth or otherwise of his allegations.

Given the earlier effort made during Charles's
presence in the narrative to establish him as a sincere
man of great moral fibre, the text should encounter no
great difficulties in completely dismissing Chris Page's
accusations that Charles was a Russian spy. Nick, for
example, as the 'wise' person of the text, could have
been used to settle the question definitively, but instead
'there was, Kelly thought, in his tone and glance, just
the faintest shade of doubt', [53] and Kelly herself is not
convinced of her dead husband's innocence. The
epilogue does attempt to restore everything and
everyone neatly back into position: the household of
women has broken up and their house itself has been
sold, Laura returns to the family home in Australia,
telling her stepmother Kelly that 'whatever I try to do,
Pentland will always be the base, the first concern, as it
was with Grandfather. Pentland, and the children Ben
and I will have.' [54] In continuing the line and family
tradition, Laura is smoothly settled back into the 'long-
view' perspective, as is Kelly in her marriage to Peter
and her return to the country.

Yet this movement towards a massive recuperation
is curiously undermined by Kelly's refusal of knowledge
regarding Charles's past:

The filing cabinets and all the papers had been taken
by removal men down Wychwood, and she and
Peter had burned every single item without reading
any of them. They would never know if what Chris
Page had said on that dreadful night contained any
truth. They did not want to know.[55]

This last lingering doubt and inconclusiveness which
closes the text – the simultaneous disclosure and
disavowal of Charles's treachery – undermines his
status as both a perfect family man and an exemplary
independent Conservative. The text's vision of
Conservatism as a moral discourse which transcends
the conflicts of social and political power in the name
of patriotism, charitableness and moral rectitude,
national consensus and the family has rested on this
earlier representation of Charles. The knowledge of his
betrayals – of family, class and nation – which is at
once acknowledged and denied, is also the knowledge
of the realities of violence, self-contradiction, exploitation and duplicity which have to be repressed if the
text is to maintain its vision of a magically unified and
stable Conservative Britain. The text's attempt to
preserve the family as a space beyond social and
political conflict is finally frustrated by this troubling of
the family which is also a troubling of the text's
conception of social and political order as a whole.

I have tried to show how the popular family saga
attempts the representation of ideological contradictions
in a form which provides their imaginary resolution,
and that this takes place through a fiction which
entertains and exposes contradiction on one condition,
that of final unity and reconciliation. This process is
both aided and impeded by the double-edged discourse
of the family, tradition, heritage, the 'long-view',
which on the one hand provides a secure foundation

from which to interrogate short-term practices, and on the other renders any attempt to follow the reassuring pattern of classical narrative (that of an original settlement disrupted and finally restored) deeply problematic.

The analysis of romance fiction has happily moved beyond that earlier phase in which the genre was righteously denounced for its facile and yet (strangely) coercive ideological effects, an analysis which brought with it the image of women readers as the passive consumers of a discourse which could only further their oppression. The necessary re-reading of romance has produced an understanding of the genre which exposes the crudity of that earlier model and its underlying assumptions about the relationship between texts and women reading. If the implications of this process of re-definition are to be drawn out fully, it needs to extend outside romance to those associated but distinct genres of which the family saga is one important instance. By attempting to situate romance within the broader field of women's reading, we can move towards not only a clearer definition of romance in its relationships of affiliation and difference with other genres, but also an understanding of the range and variety of the interactions between texts and women readers.

Acknowledgments

Thanks to Helen Birch and Barry Taylor.

Notes

1 A. Jones, 'Mills & Boon meets feminism', paper given at History Workshop Popular Fiction Conference, 1984.
2 For two influential expositions of the idea of classic realism, see Catherine Belsey, *Critical Practice*, London, Methuen, 1981,

ch.3, and Colin McCabe, 'Principles of realism and pleasure', *Screen* 17, Autumn 1976.

3 D. Steele, *Thurston House*, London, Sphere, 1983.

4 S. Howatch, *Penmarric*, London, Hamish Hamilton, 1971.

5 C. Gaskin, *Family Affairs*, Glasgow, Collins, 1980.

6 C. McCullough, *The Thorn Birds*, London, Futura, 1977.

7 J. Saxton, *The Pride*, London, Hamlyn, 1981, Preface.

8 Ibid., Preface.

9 M. Mosco, *Almonds and Raisins*, Sevenoaks, New English Library, 1979.

10 M. Swindells, *Summer Harvest*, London, Futura, 1983.

11 B. Jagger, *Flint and Roses*, London, Futura, 1982.

12 S. Heath, *Questions of Cinema*, London, Macmillan, 1981, p.125.

13 This can also be seen to operate in television sagas such as *Dallas* and *Dynasty*.

14 L.S. Robinson, *Sex, Class and Culture*, Bloomington, Indiana University Press, 1978, pp.200–6.

15 McCullough, op.cit., p.455.

16 Ibid., p.578.

17 Ibid., pp.360, 438, 362, 358.

18 Ibid., p.591.

19 Ibid.

20 Ibid.

21 Ibid.

22 Ibid.

23 Ibid.

24 Ibid.

25 Ibid.

26 Ibid.

27 Ibid.

28 Ibid.

29 Robinson, op.cit., p.202.

30 Howatch, op.cit., p.11.

31 Ibid., p.88.

32 Ibid., p.174.

33 Ibid., p.191.

34 Ibid.

35 Ibid., p.232.

36 Ibid.

37 Ibid., p.671

38 Ibid., p.233.

39 Gaskin, op.cit., p.23.

40 Ibid., p.83

41 Ibid., p.125.

42 As Alison Light points out ('Romance fiction, sexuality and class', *Feminist Review*, no.16, 1984), all fictions involve the exploration and production of desires which may be in excess of the socially possible, and the typical family saga hero certainly indicates a striving towards an imaginary control of the uncontrollable. The adoration of the powerful male in the family saga resembles the adoration of the father by the small child recognisable as the paradigmatic relationship underlying the fiction of popular romance, but the saga hero is a father figure with a difference. Displaying very little of the authoritarianism and emotional distance typical of the romance hero, he is usually open and supportive, interested in children and clothes, feelings and cooking. His willed self-involvement in the normally tabooed female rites of menstruation, pregnancy and childbirth constitutes a certain disturbance in the fixed positions of masculinity and femininity, and yet perhaps this is only possible because the power the family saga hero wields in the public world in terms of wealth, title, class and age creates a space for the indulgence of 'female' attributes in the privatised areas of home, family, children, women and sexuality.

43 Gaskin, op.cit., p.88.

44 Ibid., p.94.

45 Ibid.

46 Ibid., p.176.

47 Ibid., p.92.

48 Ibid., p.189.

49 Ibid., p.385.

50 Ibid., p.391.

51 Ibid., p.442.

52 Ibid., p.331.

53 Ibid., p.491.

54 Ibid., p.510.

55 Ibid., p.511.

Mills & Boon (1985), 'a new romance for today's woman'

9
Mills & Boon meets feminism

ANN ROSALIND JONES

Charlotte Lamb, a writer of popular romances, wrote in the *Guardian* in 1982:

> Over the past decade, the rise of feminism has been paralleled almost exactly by a mushroom growth in the popularity of romance fiction. Last year alone 250 million women bought a Mills and Boon book, in countries ranging from France to Japan, from America to Australia. (quoted in Coward, 1984: 191)

The essay that follows is a sequel to recent feminist studies of these women, the regular consumers of romance and of the pleasures they find in reading the novels that Mills & Boon and a dozen other publishing houses put on sale every month (Hay, 1983; Radway, 1983; Light, 1984; Coward, 1984). I first became interested in romance through discussing analyses of Mills & Boon novels with students in a twentieth-century literature course at the University of Sussex, but I must admit that my curiosity about popular writing aimed at women is more than academic. My first job, after I got what looked as though it was going to be a perfectly useless MA in English, was as an editorial assistant at a New York City publishing company called Dauntless Books. In 1969, Dauntless Books put out six monthly confession magazines. Their format was the story told by a heroine who tries some sexual adventuring, discovers how dangerous it is and how misled she has been, and returns to her parents or her husband a wiser and better woman.

The working population at Dauntless was bizarre, to say the least. There was the boss, a fat entrepreneur who wore spats, smoked cigars and pinched his secretary; a senior editor, a capable, tight-lipped woman whose private life was a well-kept secret but certainly wasn't centered around men; a managing editor, a divorcee after a year of marriage in the 1930s, approaching retirement and longing to escape from a world which seemed to be going mad; and five 'girls,' from 18 to 25, who made up the rousing titles and steamy photographs with which the magazines were given sex appeal. It struck me even at the time as amazing that we as a group were telling women how to live their lives – because that is what the magazines did. They paid formula writers to use the trendiest local color and most sensational news at hand to reinforce a sexual morality that dated back to Eisenhower's 1950s. East Village hippies, rock musicians and the psychedelic sub-culture in general were big in 1969; so were therapists, as the ultimate authorities to which heroines turned at the end of the stories (ministers had earlier been assigned this role). But the readers' letters that came into the office suggested that we were responding to present needs as well as purveying reactionary ideology. One of these must have been the need to be reassured that conventional morality was still worth following. If the 1960s had brought new sexual permissiveness to the urban middle class, they had brought curiosity about those changes but also deep uncertainty about the risks they entailed to the small-town, working-class women whom Dauntless targeted as readers. One woman wrote in to say that she told her daughters to read every issue of *Revealing Romances*, because they could find out from the stories what life was really like. It's not entirely clear that the message of repentance was what those daughters took away from the magazine; the exotic venues and erotic heights reached by the heroines may have been the main appeal. But young women wrote in, too, to thank us for 'exciting stories that tell it like it is.'

Dauntless Books folded in 1971. But Mills & Boon has obviously evolved a formula that combines pleasure with an acceptable level of realism in a successful way. Because such thoughtful empirical and psychoanalytic study has been done on the audience for romance, I am going to concentrate instead on the novels as texts. The main reason for this focus is that, reading them recently, I have confronted the most recent trends in the genre. I was astonished to find that every novel I read (sixteen, all published in 1983–4) either refers explicitly to feminism or deals implicitly with issues feminism has raised: women's work, their economic and psychic independence from men, their sexuality – or what might better be called the shifts in 'manners' around heterosexual attraction and pursuit. Popular literary convention is facing a new political rival.

Interesting theoretical questions also arise when formula writing confronts a changing social context. To what extent does the genre retain its central features? To what extent do writers adapt to new economic and ideological currents? How far can the genre change without collapsing into a new form? Romance has been a persistently popular mode in western literature: lovers have met, separated and been blissfully reunited since Alexandrian Greece, as in Longus' *Daphnis and Chloe*, in the Roman comic theater, in Arthurian cycles, Italian pastoral, and throughout the popular as well as now canonized psychological/realist novels of the eighteenth and nineteenth centuries. But it is only recently that romance has been aimed so exclusively at women. It was written and read by aristocrats of both sexes until the eighteenth century; only then did it begin to be mocked as a feminine preoccupation. Its specifically feminine readership in the 1980s is determined not only by cultural habit but by a concerted program of market research, mass publication and multi-media advertising. So the question is more than theoretical. What happens when a mega-industry geared toward women in traditional roles confronts a political movement opposed to the basic premises on which its books are written? In this corner, Mills & Boon and the faith that a woman's greatest happiness lies in love and marriage; in that corner, feminism, which questions the social construction of that faith and the viability of that institution.

As a basis for analysing the ideological turmoil that Mills & Boon novels now reveal, let me offer a summary of a typical romance plot, as it's been stabilized in the genre and is still used by older writers. The heroine, a virgin in her early twenties, is set in a social limbo: her family is dead or invisible, her friends are few or none, her occupational milieu is only vaguely filled in. As a result, her meeting with the hero occurs in a private realm which excludes all concerns but their mutual attraction; the rest of the world drops away except as a backdrop (often exotic and luxurious, defined through the hero's wealth and taste). The hero, seven to ten years older than the heroine, is dazzlingly successful in the public world; in private life, he is a rake or a mystery, saturnine in appearance, sexually expert, and relentlessly domineering. He takes the reins erotically, naming the heroine's desires to her ('You know you want me, why resist?'); all she can do is submit or flee. She tries constantly to interpret his behavior, which alternates abruptly between tenderness

and rejection. Finally, after a separation, the hero
tracks the heroine down, explains his earlier motives
and offers her love and marriage. They fall into a final
embrace (at Dauntless, it was called 'the clinch') which,
for decency's sake, is often interrupted by a final
delaying line: 'Let's go tell your mother,' or 'Wait, my
love, let's save the ultimate ecstasy for our wedding
night.'

I am not the first to point out that this formula is
neither as absurd nor as rigid as it seems. Feminist
analysis of romance has refused to condemn its
audience as passive, escapist victims of mass publishing.
Contrary to David Margolies's dismissal of romance
readers' tendency to 'sink into feeling' (Margolies,
1982:9), Janice Radway has discovered that romance
audiences read actively: they reject certain novels,
recommend others to each other, know how to find
writers and heroines who appeal to them (Radway,
1983: 63–4). The concentration on courtship –
on premarital pursuit and resistance – has been
recognized by feminists as an affirmation of the one
period of women's lives when social consensus puts
their concerns at center stage: the novels focus on the
critical moment when the heroines' survival skills are
put to the test, when their ability to negotiate the
conflict between male desire and long-term commitment (between the status of 'slag' and 'drag,' as Valerie
Hay charts them, using Celia Cowie and Sue Lees's
study of working-class girls' dilemmas, Hay, 1873: 15)
leads them to emotional triumph and economic
security. The hero must say 'I love you' and he must
say 'Marry me.' There is nothing fantastic in this
privileging of the preliminaries to marriage. As Hay
writes, 'It is possible to read romance as a survival
manual in a world in which women's right to romance
is legitimated as being one of the few "rights" to
anything that women have'. (16) And the frequent

interruption of sex scenes, like the overall delaying structure of the plot, may well correspond to many women's experience of sex as better in anticipation than in action. A line mid-way through a 1984 Mills & Boon suggests the importance of eros as anticipation: 'She wanted the moment to last forever, so that he would always be coming toward her and she waiting for him' (Sandra Field, *A Mistake in Identity*: 83). As Alison Light puts it, 'The reader is left in a permanent state of foreplay, but I would guess that for many women this is the best heterosexual sex they ever get' (Light, 1984:23).

Feminists analysing romance have also pointed out that the masculine and feminine roles suggested in a standard plot summary are not so simple. The hero is never finally represented as being as brutal as he may at first appear to be; the heroine is fulfilled not through his cruelty but through his transformation. The turning point of the novel is often a moment of collapse through which power relations are reversed. If the heroine collapses (falls, faints, gets sick), the hero is turned into a gently nurturing figure. Rosalind Coward argues that this turnabout appeals to feminine Oedipal fantasies of winning one's father as lover (Coward, 1984: 195); Janice Radway sees it as fulfilling the desire to be mothered again (Radway, 1983: 62). One novelist covers every familial possibility, including sibling desire: the heroine is compared first to 'a little girl being administered to by her father,' then to 'a small child being helped by an older brother,' and finally to 'a baby,' whom the hero tucks under the covers 'as lovingly as any mother' (Amanda Carpenter, *The Wall*). Scenes in which the heroine is held, rocked, fed, bathed and doctored are very common; the narrative emphasizes the hero's unsuspected skills as caretaker rather than seducer, and the heroine is positioned not as victim but as the center of expert care and attention. If the hero collapses, his temporary helplessness reverses whatever master/slave combat the preceding narrative has set up, while the heroine's response to the emergency represents her as cool-headed, capable, even heroic. She drags him a quarter mile out of a sinking boat (*Identity*), or, at the least, her conventional domestic skills can be shown as effective beyond the private realm: as hostess, she saves a diplomatic occasion (Rachel Lindsay, *Forbidden Love*); as secretary, she restores her boss to competence (Yvonne' Whittal, *Ride the Wind*). Without any direct reference to feminism, the standard romance plot may nevertheless reconstruct relations between the sexes. By page 140 of the required 180, nurturant men and competent women occupy test situations that super-sede conventional gender roles.

But overt references to feminism are much more problematic in Mills & Boon. The term itself, like the demands and debates associated with it, produces striking ambivalence in these novels, even when they register changes that are feminist in effect. A similar suppression of the political often surfaces in 'liberal' magazines in which women are asked to comment on their views of feminism. A typical response is 'I support equal pay for equal work, of course, but spare me any connection with those unattractive extremists' (see, for several versions of this position, *Options*, June 1984, 'Who me, a feminist?'). What happens is that certain positions put foward by feminism are taken for granted, along with the economic and ideological benefits it has brought many women, while the movement itself is perceived as alien, threatening, excessive. Many Mills & Boon heroines work, travel and cope on their own, but they are assigned lines of defense (and revealingly confused syntax) such as 'Just because I have my kind of job, it doesn't make me any less of a woman' (Ann Cooper, *Maelstrom*: 120) or

'Because I believe in sexual equality, it doesn't mean I'm against marriage and the family' (Kay Clifford, *The Duke Wore Jeans*: 68).

The balance is often less delicate than this. At one extreme, Mills & Boon uses feminism in mocking or antithetical ways, to initiate a counter-movement. A frequent instance is the hero's deliberate misinterpretation of what the heroine says (the old 'you sure are pretty when you're mad' routine). The writer assigns the heroine a defense of her independence; she then assigns the hero a speech in which he diverts the heroine's declaration into a sexual come-on.

> 'You don't own me,' she flung recklessly. . . .
> 'I'm a woman, not a toy!'
> 'I know you're a woman,' he said, his voice suddenly filled with passion.
> Her heart forced itself against her breast, until she was almost suffocating. (Charlotte Lamb, *The Cruel Flame*: 57)

The last sentence in this passage is especially significant: the challenge to conventional sexual expectations voiced by the heroine becomes the occasion for their reinforcement in the narrative. She can be feminist *and* sexy.

A particularly sinister appropriation of feminist politics to eroticize a male/female scene involves jokes or threats related to rape. One writer increases the suspense of a bedroom scene by assigning the estranged wife this line: 'There's now a law that forbids a man to rape his wife – just in case you didn't know.' The narrative continues: 'Her words seemed to have no effect on him at all, he simply walked around the bed, still watching her, still studying her' (Penny Jordan, *Shadow Marriage*: 107). Feminism, that is, is referred to in ways that suggest it has produced dangers it cannot allay. Further instances: a hero attributes a heroine's flippant rejection of marriage to her reading of 'too many feminist magazines' (Sally Wentworth, *Backfire*: 73); a heroine travelling to America concludes, with conservative cheerfulness, 'Whoever had said that the American male was losing his libido because of female domination had obviously not visited California recently' (*Duke*: 26). This misrepresentation via abridgment is akin to the procedure by which feminists are invited onto TV talk shows but denied the conceptual space and air time in which to make their positions clear.

Roland Barthes, in *Mythologies*, describes what he calls the 'inoculation effect' (Barthes, 1972:41–2,150) in mass culture: an institutional discourse admits the possibility that the institution is liable to criticism, but the allusion to the critique actually functions to reinforce the status quo. The defense is phrased as 'yes, but': 'yes the army's not perfect, but. . . ; yes, heterosexual courtship involves some inequities, but. . . .' The critique is cited and taken over in ways that deflate its power. One Mills & Boon hero manages to admit his anti-feminism and to turn it into a virtue (frank speaking) at the same time:

> 'You really are a chauvinist pig, aren't you?' she snapped.
> 'Most men are. But they haven't the guts to say so.' (*Duke*, 69)

A suspicious reader, considering the mass audience presumably addicted to the happy ending in which marriage solves all problems, might argue that the Mills & Boon novel is generically bound to treat feminism in this way. Romance can afford a flirtation with feminism: the genre game is already won.

But what is striking in these novels is not a smooth

recuperation of feminism. On the contrary, what I have noticed in them is their multi-leveled incoherence in dealing with it. Few writers, to judge from recent novels, can ignore feminism; but none can work out a seamless fit between the claims of modern women and the old rib-bones of romance: the demand to be employed in a job worth a lifetime's concentration and to be loved, to be gratified as a working and desiring subject, sits uneasily with the prevailing convention through which the miraculous appearance of a man whose worldly millions and erotic genius solve all problems of identity and pleasure for the heroine once he admits that she is his one and only love. The conflict between feminism as emergent ideology and romance as residual genre produces three kinds of contradiction: narrative discontinuity, irreconcilable settings, and inconsistency in realist dialogue. I'm not arguing that Mills & Boon readers do, don't or should notice these contradictions, or that they are much bothered by them if they do notice them: the pleasures of these texts lie elsewhere. But if the novels are read symptomatically, as evidence of ideological conflict producing disturbances in the conventions of popular realism, I think they pose important questions about writing and reading in a socio-literary climate influenced by feminism, so far, in partial and touchy ways.

On the level of plots, the novels seem to try to have it both ways – first the new, then the old. After long or repeated passages representing the heroine's capacities and ambitions outside marriage, the ending almost inevitably assigns her a future defined by the needs of the hero. A case in point: the hero, an Australian cane grower, convinces the heroine to leave her teaching job and come back with him to the plantation where his father is dying. As she arrives, she is overwhelmed by dynastic loyalty to his family: 'And there would be children – Mitch would want a son to inherit the vast acreage of Ballantyne cane' (Helen Bianchin, *The Hills of Home*: 24). Predictably, the heroine is chosen to supply this heir. References to the financial independence and the city life she has staunchly defended disappear after the first fifty pages, while the phrasing of the conclusion suggests that her progress from working girl to wife has been splendidly inevitable: the final embrace leaves her 'secure in the knowledge that he was her reason for living – that together they belonged, almost as if fate itself had decreed it.'

At times, contradictory character positions are more obvious because they are juxtaposed more abruptly. The heroine shifts suddenly from a moment of confident autonomy to blind confusion at the appearance of the hero, and the narrative supports his version of the scene and of the heroine, in flat contradiction to what has been represented immediately before. One heroine, standing in the surf, pulls herself together:

> Her loneliness suddenly made her feel happy. It was good for her; it would teach her about herself.
> She wanted to paint this scene . . . this tiny unfriendly bay. Tomorrow she would go to the nearest town and buy some paints, some paper.

But five paragraphs further on, the hero is warning her that the terrain is too much for her – which she concedes, as though her earlier moment of lucidity and decision had never occurred:

> 'It can be dangerous along here.'
> 'I can look after myself.'
> 'Can you? You're wandering about like a lost child!'. . . . She knew that all too well, but she wasn't about to admit it to him. (Patricia Lake, *Illusion of Love*: 52–3)

Sometimes the tension between representing the heroine's self-sufficiency and reasserting her need for the hero is so great that the effect is unintentionally comic:

> It could have been anybody, any man, but it had been Luke who had ripped the veils from her eyes and forced her to face up to the reality of life as a grown woman. She put her head in her hands and began to sob like a baby. (*Illusion*: 101)

The ending of this novel rehearses the same opposition between independent competence and helpless need; again, the interpretation the heroine gives to events rewrites the prior narrative of autonomy. Fleeing the hero, she starts work as a bartender/waitress in a friend's restaurant on the Riviera: 'She picked up the work easily, her fluency in French being a great help. And she had to admit that she was enjoying it' (155). But the hero appears, takes her to bed, and so overwhelms her that only his practised handling of the morning-after awkwardness moves the story on to the happy ending: 'It was all thanks to Luke's control of the situation. . . . "I love you," he told her. It was all she would ever need to know, it was everything she wanted.'

At its most recuperative, Mills & Boon uses women's work merely cosmetically, to construct a glamorous opening identity for its heroines: they are actresses, singers, lawyers, public relations consultants, advertising designers. But when the romantic plot begins to thicken, the jobs appear with implausible rapidity, through devices that undermine the series' general effort toward verisimilitude. (Writers for Mills & Boon are warned that consistency in character-ization and accuracy of setting are essential, but job duties in a specific workplace seem to be disposable ingredients in this characterization.) Heroes or other men advancing their interests manipulate the heroine's employment without her knowledge and with incredible ease: agents are bribed, posts are found abroad, fierce headmistresses are charmed, leaves of absence are immediately available when the heroine needs time to track the hero down, or, more often, to wait for him to find her in a lyrical setting and to propose. Romance, in order to negotiate the actual contradictions between absorbing work and total dedication to a man, must contradict its own claims to realism. For the love conflict to occupy center stage, the job that gives the heroine glamor must always be temporary.

A second kind of contradiction involves the placement of an individualistic, proto-feminist heroine in class and national settings through which she is absorbed into a nostalgic or reactionary social position. The dynastic novel reappears in this category: stately homes and noble family lines elicit the heroine's loyalty and protection, although she rarely has a kinship link to them. The strain in these novels is that heroines who start out as representatives of at least a mild 1980s progressivism must be made to turn out as dutiful daughters to the past. Their careers and psychic comfort must be sacrificed for a greater cause, often a fantasized traditional Englishness that requires pages of tender description. The go-getting lawyer heroine of *The Duke Wore Jeans*, for example, tolerates the boorishness of an American playboy partly because she hopes she can influence him into becoming a good (paternalistic) landlord of the five-centuries-old estate he has just inherited. In a similarly patriotic/nostalgic vein, a highly educated press agent for the British diplomatic service tolerates a demeaning position as secretary to the monstrous wife of an ambassador to Hong Kong; she holds out for the sake of queen and country – and because the ascetic, long-suffering hero incarnates the gentlemanly virtues of Empire (*Forbidden Love*). Another heroine, mocked as a Victorian and praised as a Madonna, flees swinging London to return to her native Cornish village, represented at length as preserving ancient rural values – which the TV-star hero, a local boy himself, turns out to have appreciated all along (*Flame*). In each case, the heroine's will is subordinated to a mythic past, and her reward for rejecting the modern world is marriage to a man at the top of unquestioned class and political hierarchies. Not only does the heroine's entry into upper-class family life shut down any possibility of critique of the milieu to which she rises; her success (which depends on her beauty and her persistence in old-fashioned virtues, often in contrast to a rival who is made to exemplify modern corruption) becomes a 'confirmation' of its openness and flexibility. The good old days overpower any possibility of a new women's era.

A third contradiction occurs on the level of diction, or literary register. There's often a striking dissonance between the normal density of realist dialogue and the aphoristic or proverbial mode in which traditional feminine positions are asserted. Conflicting languages are spoken: the narrator suddenly assigns eternal verities to characters whose speeches until then have been colloquial responses to local circumstances. The hero, for example, may draw back from an embrace to make a pronouncement in a vocabulary better suited to the romance narrator than to the personality she has constructed for him. A racing driver turned tough-guy actor, for example, speaks to one heroine as follows: "'That's how you should look," he told her thickly. "A woman in love looks like that – bemused, enchanted"' (*Flame*: 62). More often, the heroine is given a speech opposed to her earlier actions or statements. One instance: in *Backfire*, a novel in which the heroine has been represented as experiencing intense sexual pleasure in spite of the double-agent role she plays toward the hero, a scene is suddenly resolved with her use of an old saw about feminine modesty versus masculine lust:

> His tone changed, grew soft. . . . 'Last night was the most wonderful in my life – and will be until our wedding day,' he added.
> But he meant wedding night, Abby thought. The wedding *day* is for the woman, the *night* for the man. (*Backfire*: 142)

Generalizations of this kind are an obvious sign of tension. The heroine has gone too far; gender law and order must be restored. The compensatory process is especially evident in *Almost a Stranger*, a novel full of sharp feminist repartee and often critical of patriarchal family and work life. But even here the heroine suddenly announces, uncharacteristically, 'A woman can have lots of things to love, but she always loves children best' (103); and the hero, generally a spirited and intelligent defender of women's capabilities, announces, 'A woman's *got* to need a man' (131). I can't tell whether interpolations of this kind are the conscious work of editors or the effects of authorial unconsciousness. Judging from a conversation with a Mills & Boon editor, I would guess that they result from a deliberate compromise on the part of writers who know that they can expand the formula in feminist directions as long as they observe its basic romantic requirements. In any case, such shifts in character and dialogue are certainly evidence of ideological conflict.

Strains are also evident in the language of Mills & Boon love scenes. These no longer represent only aggressive heroes trying to weaken the resistance of a virginal heroine; romance has adopted less repressive doctrines about female sexuality, at least to the extent of constructing heroines capable of desire and even of pursuing men. But the imagery that recurs in love scenes still belongs to a discourse that links sex to nature: built into the body, eternally the same. Passion is irresistible; *therefore* it requires cautious handling and institutional containment. (Dauntless Books took exactly this line.) Critiques of the double standard are now admissible; the notion that sexuality is socially constructed, variable, re-inventable rather than instinctive is not. Orgasms in Mills & Boon are always vaginal, always single, simultaneous with the man's and experienced in missionary position; verbal conventions are equally fixed. Nature metaphors and biological determinism go hand in hand: storms of desire, floods of ecstasy are linked to 'urgent primeval passion' (*Illusion*:59); the heroine's body convulses 'in needs as old as the seasons' (*Identity*: 69); rationality is suspended as 'bodies take over from minds' (*Shadow Marriage*: 110). But the appeal to primordial drive often has a forced quality, as if the formula is in need of emphatic re-assertion. A narrative is being artifically, even rather desperately eroticized when a heroine, watching a man, must be described as noticing 'the total difference of his male shape when compared to hers' (*Shadow Marriage*) or when, in the midst of a cocktail party, she is assigned a sudden, Lawrentian fit of gestation compulsion: 'Children, Ben's children – God, how she ached to bear them! The primitiveness of her own response amazed her' (151). The old sexual fix is wearing out, beginning to sound laboured.

The kinds of contradiction I've identified can be observed in most recent romances, I think. But as a categorical framework, they also foreground what appear to be real innovations in (by my count) a third of Mills & Boon novels. It is too soon to say whether the genre is capable of major transformation, but it is clear that writers and editors are now willing to experiment in liberal-feminist directions. The positive treatment of women's demands may be a signal of deep change; perhaps it simply indicates editorial confidence that the genre can absorb enough feminism to appeal to a changing readership while still containing the movement's radical potentials, to the extent that the basic premise of the genre can go unchallenged: the greatest goal and pleasure in a woman's life is the love of a good man. But variations and expansions of that premise are certainly taking place in the Mills & Boon fantasy factory. Departures from the standard formula ought not to be exaggerated; they are not predominant in the 1983–4 novels I have read, and especially not in the earlier novels now being reprinted as 'Best Seller Romances.' But changes ought not to be dismissed as merely surface, either; if the liberal-feminist current is popular with readers, it will certainly be encouraged in future editorial policy.

One major change is that plots now sustain a heroine's commitment to her work. Even at the end of certain novels, the heroine's demand to be loved as a working woman is still heard, and it must be negotiated before the couple falls into the last embrace. Toward the end of *Maelstrom*, for example, two petroleum engineers confront each other: she insists that she will continue to work after marrying him, he leaves in a rage. But they are reunited through a compromise: she will continue in the work she's been trained for, but with a company less reckless than the one now employing her. The novel is unusually well researched (oil exploration in Saudi Arabia, the risks of well-drilling), and the crisis is genuinely exciting: the couple risks life and limb to cap an exploding well, a spectacular accomplishment which they carry out as a pair. In other novels, the heroine's dedication to her work generates the love plot: her boss recognizes her as a kindred soul, another 'workaholic' (Emma Darcy, *Tangle of Torment*), or her fame as a singer intrigues the hero, who is finally forced to admit that his neurosis rather than iron-clad dogmas of wifely subordination underlies his refusal to accept her public career (*The Wall*). In a fourth case, *Almost a Stranger*, the heroine's feminism generates plot developments unconnected to the central love story: she foments rebellion among the daughters in the family and inspires the hero to promote women in the company. The writer's critique, through the heroine, of the clotheshorse/hostess role of upper-middle-class women and of the loss of feminine brainpower in anti-woman workplaces, through the hero, is all the more striking because it is not directed strucurally toward the unfolding of the love plot.

Several novels also move beyond traditional class and nationalist values. Rather than drawing an up-to-date heroine back into feudal or Victorian settings, the writer affirms her claims to new professional and emotional territory. The five most liberal novels I've read are set not in English villages or colonies but in large cities in Commonwealth countries, the United States and Canada – fantasy frontiers – and the heroines are self-made women, anti-traditionalists whose feminism is not submerged under the hero's benevolence. The petroleum engineer parodies her eventual lover by declaring her standards for men at work: 'I don't dislike working with men . . . *if* they know their job – and if they're intelligent enough to realise that I know mine' (*Maelstrom*: 26–7); an ad designer challenges her boss to recognize the realities of sexual harassment: 'I wonder how long you'd keep a secretary who kept referring to your physique every time she handed you some papers' (*Tangle*: 17); and when the heroine of *Almost a Stranger* addresses a political analysis with a historical dimension to her grandfather, it's clear that she rejects the assumptions upon which his conglomerate has been built:

Women haven't been *allowed* to be good at
business. . . . Their problem is that it's been made
almost impossible for them in a male-dominated
world. A world, incidentally, that's in a wretched
mess. Maybe men could do with a little less
aggression. (95)

Finally, there seems to be a new emphasis in the love
scenes. The heroine lets loose her passion for the hero
deliberately, at the moment when she perceives that his
desire for her makes him as dependent on her as she is
on him. This recognition of reciprocity is often
represented as a surprisingly lucid moment; storms of
emotion may be bursting all around, but the heroine
opens both eyes and sees clearly:

He raised his head, looked into her eyes, and
she knew she was seeing to the core of the man.
He needed her now, tonight. He wanted her physically, yes . . . but emotionally he needed her.
(*The Wall*: 133)

There may even be a quality of triumph in the
heroine's recognition: 'she realised how much she had
yearned to see him like this, as much a victim of need
as she was herself' (*Shadow Marriage*: 110); or her sense
of control may be so strong that a scene reverses
conventional seducer/virgin roles: 'This was his
moment of weakness . . . the elation of power was
dancing in her veins. All she had to do was reach out
and claim him' (*Tangle*: 108–9). What these heroines
wait for is not the safety of marriage but the certainty
that the hero is as vulnerable as they are. The love
scenes position heroine and hero as *alike*. They offer a
basis of erotic equality on which the heroine takes a
calculated risk. If she gives up her virginity (most do),
she gives it to a man who is represented as equally at

risk – if not physically, at least psychically. Compensatory mechanisms are at work in these novels (the heroine of *The Wall* plays a motherly-supportive role toward the hero, the sexually aggressive heroine of *Tangle of Torment* ends up pregnant and helpless) – but a new, more liberal conception of feminine potential is none the less at work.

It seems, in fact, so difficult to assess any of these novels as regressive or progressive in its totality that I've concluded such judgments aren't the point. Taken as a group, the texts prove that the genre is flexible, but not at every point. One instance: I doubt that the romance format will ever allow writers to challenge the conventions through which the hero is constructed: he is still older, richer, wiser in the ways of the world, and more experienced sexually than the heroine. The ideology of masculinity in Mills & Boon may be more rigid (and oppressive to men) than the guidelines through which the heroines are produced. And the focus on men's power in the public realm, even if it is temporarily laid aside in the privacy of the love scenes, has other consequences for the genre. For one thing, the narrative perspective in these novels still privileges the male gaze: the hero's perspective is always the one from which the heroine's looks are described. Or, in a feminine variation of the gaze, heroines stare into mirrors, in long auto-erotic scenes of dressing and making-up that reinforce the pragmatic narcissism in which women are trained as objects of desire. Another result of the centrality of the hero is that woman-to-woman relationships are tangential or fraught; although some novels represent strong families, including energetic and capable mothers, the heroine is more likely to be given a woman friend as a merely temporary confidante – or to confront heartless or amoral rivals for the hero's love. Most important, is a romance ever likely to question the ultimate value of marriage? Failed marriages are often the starting point for a novel, but the plot works to re-eroticize the estranged couple by confirming the irresistible attraction between them and removing the misunderstandings that caused the first breach. As the failure of a series of ambiguously ended novels proves, the happy ending is not up for revision.

Rather than dismissing Mills & Boon for the ossification of its formula, however, we might pose the issue the other way around: what questions does the success of the genre raise to proponents of a more progressive women's fiction? Simply put, what's wrong with a happy ending? What kind might a genuinely feminist novel offer? Slammed doors, or doors opened tentatively onto uncertain futures seem to be the pattern for feminist endings; is a more utopian mode imaginable in 1986? If it were, would 250 million women want to read it? How successful might a hybrid novel combining feminist depth of analysis with a plausibly positive ending be? Is such a hybrid possible? How important is it for feminists to set up alternatives to popular publishing – or is the best strategy now one of genre-subversion, of stealing into mass markets via temporary literary camouflage? Which changes first, writers, audiences, or editors? What is the role of literary agents, publishers, reviewers? How fast can generic changes occur? Are they necessarily blurred and recuperative to begin with?

Whatever the answers, I would argue that the changes occurring now in Mills & Boon suggest what a popular women's novel is likely to be for a long time to come, given the economic, social and psychic forces that continue to make the ideally matched couple look to many readers like the still center of a spinning universe. But it seems a promising sign that romance also represents that universe as expanding. The narrative interest accorded to women's work outside the household, the critique of male supremacy in the office and the bedroom, some notion that masculine and feminine desire may not be light years apart, or fixed for eternity – these are certainly signs of life stirring in (up?) an ancient literary mode. The politics of gender have already become a politics of genre.

Recent studies of romance

Batsleer, Janet (1981), 'Pulp in the pink,' *Spare Rib*, no. 109 (August).

Coward, Rosalind (1984), 'Overwhelming desire,' *Female Desire: Women's Sexuality Today*, London: Paladin.

Douglas, Ann (1980), 'Soft-porn culture,' *The New Republic* (30 August).

English Studies Group, Birmingham Centre for Contemporary Cultural Studies (1980), 'Recent developments in English Studies at the Centre (Work in Progress, no. 2),' *Culture, Media, Language: Working Papers in Cultural Studies*, London: Birmingham CCCS/Hutchinson.

Harrison, Rachel (1978), '*Shirley*: relations of reproduction and the ideology of romance,' *Women Take Issue*, London: Women's Studies Group, Birmingham CCCS/Hutchinson.

Hay, Valerie (1983), 'The necessity of romance,' *Women's Studies Occasional Papers*, no. 3, Canterbury: University of Kent.

Light, Alison (1984), 'Returning to Manderley – romance fiction, female sexuality and class,' *Feminist Review*, no. 16 (Summer).

Margolies, David (1982), 'Mills and Boon – guilt without sex,' *Red Letters*, no. 14.

Modleski, Tina (1980), 'The disappearing act: a study of Harlequin romances,' *Signs*, 5, 1 (Autumn).

Radway, Janice (1983), 'Women read the romance,' *Feminist Studies*, 9, 1 (Spring).

Radway, Janice (1984), *Reading the Romance*, Chapel Hill, North Carolina, University of North Carolina Press.

Robinson, Lilian (1978), 'On reading trash,' *Sex, Class and Culture*, Bloomington and London: Indiana University Press.

Snitow, Ann (1979/1984), 'Mass market romances: pornography

for women is different,' *Radical History Review*, no. 20 (Spring/
Summer), reprinted in *Desire: The Politics of Sexuality*,
ed. Ann Snitow,   Christine Stansell   and   Sharon Thompson,
London: Virago.

Related studies

Barthes, Roland (1972), *Mythologies*, London: Jonathan Cape.
Davies, Tony (1983), 'Transports of pleasure: fiction and its
   audiences in the later nineteenth century,' *Formations of Pleasure*,
   London: Routledge & Kegan Paul.
McRobbie, Angela (1978), 'Jackie: an ideology of adolescent
   femininity,' CCCS Stencilled Paper no. 53.
Sharratt, Norma (1983), 'Girls, jobs and glamour,' *Feminist Review*,
   no. 15 (Winter).

Mills & Boon romances, winter 1983–spring 1984

Bianchin, Helen, *The Hills of Home* (Best Seller Romance) Heroine
   marries for the sake of hero's dying father, on the family
   plantation in Australia.
Carpenter, Amanda, *The Wall* Singing star on vacation meets
   recluse hero, convinces him that she'll go on with her career
   (Midwest, USA).
Clifford, Kay, *The Duke Wore Jeans* London lawyer discovers the
   virtues of American *Playboy* editor, and of his English mansion,
   recently inherited.
Cooper, Ann, *Maelstrom* Petroleum engineer in Saudi Arabia holds
   out for continued career against co-worker hero.
Darcy, Emma, *Tangle of Torment* Advertising designer pursues her
   would-be detached boss (Sydney).
Field, Sandra, *A Mistake in Identity* Ex-ski champion, now
   bookstore owner in Montreal, is kidnapped by the hero, who
   thinks she's a drug-pusher who's betrayed his brother.
Fraser, Alison, *The Price of Freedom* Young mother of an
   illegitimate son is sought out by her ex-lover's brother
   (Scotland/London).
Hilton, Margery, *The Dark Side of Marriage* (Best Seller Romance)
   Heroine fakes wedded bliss with her estranged husband, for the
   sake of his dying mother (London/Yorkshire).

Jordan, Penny, *Shadow Marriage* Estranged actress is reconciled to her director husband during filming (London/Spain).

Lake, Patricia, *Illusion of Love* Heroine clears up her father's debts and marries the British tycoon who pays them (Hawaii/British coast).

Lamb, Charlotte, *The Cruel Flame* (Best Seller Romance) Heroine wins TV actor, both from Cornish village (via London).

Lindsay, Rachel, *Forbidden Love* (Best Seller Romance) Diplomatic corps heroine saves ambassador from his alcoholic wife and from Russian espionage (Hong Kong).

Mather, Anne, *Sirocco* Legal secretary is kidnapped by French/Arabian millionaire (London/Iran).

Way, Margaret, *Almost a Stranger* Feminist heroine finds misogyny and love in her grandfather's firm (Sydney).

Wentworth, Sally, *Backfire* Actress falls in love with the tycoon she's been hired to spy on (London).

Whittal, Yvonne, *Ride the Wind* Secretary helps her boss through his resistance to marriage (Australia).

Portrait of Christine de Pisan, Illuminated Manuscript (British Library)

10

Write, she said

MICHELE ROBERTS

I have great difficulty starting and finishing pieces of writing. I've brought this one away with me to Italy in order to restart it. I've already torn up three rough drafts.

I'm sitting in the hot garden of a seventeenth century house, a mountain at my back and an abyss just beyond the gate; I've no access to libraries or to reference books. But this *is* a possible site for romance. Desire, I decide, is the key to unlocking the flow of words. I've always wanted to be able to talk to Christine de Pisan,† and here she is, sitting opposite me in the shade of a huge blue lavender bush fizzing with bees.

MR: Christine, I've been asked to write about why a woman author would want to write in the romance form. What do *you* think?
CP: To make money, I suppose. To make a living.
MR: But why choose that particular form? She might make better money writing thrillers, for example.
CP: Isn't it rather arrogant of you, Michele, to think you can find an answer to this question when you

†Christine de Pisan (c.1364–1430) was the fourteenth century Italian writer who wrote *La Cité des Dames*, a treatise on women's education, and much prose and poetry on the theme of love, before entering a convent where she died. She also wrote a passionate defence of women in reply to Jean de Meung's attack in *Roman de la Rose*.

221

don't write romances yourself? At least, you like to think you don't. You're rather a snob, you know: you prefer to call what *you* write *novels*. *Literature*. As a result you reify the current conventional distinction between high-class and low-class forms and avoid recognizing your debt to a distinct female literary tradition.

MR: Hang on a minute. That's not completely true. Let me explain. Actually I'm beginning to get fed up with true confessions, my own especially, as a feminist fictional form. But I'll readily admit to you that I've been an avid reader of romances in my time. In secret of course. At the peak of my lust, when I was about 14, I thought that only housewives read romances, and that since housewives were considered an inferior species of humanity engaged in boring and worthless work their leisure pursuits must be equally trivial and banal. I didn't want to be counted as one of them. And when I was at university, the books I scattered oh so carelessly around my room were by great male authors such as Balzac and Zola. Then one day my grandmother innocently blew the gaff when she remarked to some friends I'd brought home and wanted to impress, 'Oh yes, Mimi's a great reader, and your favourite author's Georgette Heyer, isn't she, dear?'

CP: So you were found out, you hypocrite!

MR: Yes. Then some years later, as a result of becoming a feminist and needing to question the common sense assumptions that shaped my life, I started wondering why it was apparently all right to enjoy reading Jane Austen and the Brontës and Mrs Gaskell but not the twentieth century novels their works subsequently inspired. Well, of course I knew a lot of men who couldn't bear reading women authors at all, not even the ones like Emily Brontë who at least had a place in the male pantheon of Great Writers. But, amongst women, there seemed to be some anxiety.

Emily's description of the wuthering heights of passion had more status than Victoria's Holt's. Charlotte's lovelorn governess had more class than Georgette Heyer's. Yet often, the story and the plot were the same. My reasons for reading them were the same: I was hungry, greedy, for a feast of words. I also read cornflake packets and seed catalogues and *The Story of O*. Was it simply a matter of class distinction? That the work of Emily and Charlotte represented what I'd been taught at university to think of as *good food* whereas that of Victoria and Georgette represented *junk*, in the same way that working class people are criticized for not eating expensive health foods? Were literary judgments based on snobbery? And if so, wasn't it simply inverted snobbery for highly educated feminists to claim, as I heard some do, that they simply adored campy old Cartland? A form of slumming? Oh dear I do feel guilty saying this I'm just as elitist as all those male critics I affect to despise.

CP: Jane Austen pokes fun at all this literary snobbery in *Northanger Abbey*. You remember that bit where Henry Tilney teases Catherine for not being able adequately to defend her love of romantic thrillers and mysteries? Oh, it's only a novel, he mimics the young lady apologizing as she lays it down hastily. I sympathize with Catherine very much when she confesses she doesn't like reading history because there are so few women in it. I myself, you know, wrote *The City of Women*, which you could argue is one of the precursors of the modern novel, precisely in order to put the women back into history, as well as to alter their representation in literature.

MR: I wouldn't call *The City of Women* a romance, exactly.

CP: No. I've always had problems with the romance form. Take Jean de Meung's *Roman de la Rose*. When I first read it I was absolutely infuriated by its misogyny, the sharp distinctions the author makes between pure women and bad women, the way women are blamed for distracting the hero from his high holy quest. I wrote a long work attacking it.

MR: In modern times, the romance is seen as a feminine form, written by and for women. In your day was the romance a male form?

CP: Not in any inherent sense. If a woman starts thinking like that, seeing the romance as only for men to write, how could she ever write one? She might as well give up immediately. No. Plenty of women wrote romances, and wrote them in the way they wanted to. But what struck me when I read the *Roman de la Rose* and then re-read all the romancers I so enjoyed in my youth, such as Chrétien de Troyes, was how, for these male authors, there was always a male hero at the centre of the story with the woman on the sidelines. She represented his eventual reward, or his soul, and so forth. I was dissatisfied with this. I wanted to write works in which the action revolved around women. But I was still able to stay with the forms I inherited, the allegorical method and so on. The world of our romances was a male-dominated one, in which the chivalric relationships between men were often the most important thing. Well, I wasn't going to deny the worth of chivalric ideals! But I *did* want to extend them to women, to argue that women were just as capable as men of loyalty to codes of honour and noble behaviour and so on.

MR: One of the most attractive features the medieval romance offers its author is the possibility of creating a very broad fictional landscape. You can decide to jump into a leather coracle and set sail for heaven, you can explore the earthly paradise with its talking birds and mountains of glass, you can struggle through primeval forests peopled with whole bestiaries of fabulous monsters, you can leap from the court of King Arthur to the very edge of the known world, you're allowed to describe the passage of time of hundreds of years.

CP: Medieval magical realism? Maybe it's a similar landscape to what you call the unconscious nowadays? But don't forget, all the same, that we were working within formal constraints. All the motifs you mention are conventional ones. They occur over and over again, even if the pattern changes a little each time. They may be archetypes, but they are historically fixed. We weren't quite as wild and free as you suggest. We used our sources well!

MR: If I were to write a modern romance I'd be using conventional motifs too: the exotic setting, let's say a chateau in Provence or an Italian country house like this one here or a castle in the Scottish highlands; the beautiful orphan girl; the sexually brutal but fundamentally tender hero; the misunderstanding that almost separates them for ever; their final blissful reunion.

CP: The modern hero has changed. He more openly represents what I believe you call the id? Heathcliff and Mr Rochester have replaced Sir Perceval. Sir Tristram and Sir Lancelot are always shown as idealizing women, even when they're committing adultery with them.

MR: Not only the idea of the hero has changed. I think the whole emotional world of the romance has altered. It's narrowed. The modern heroine may well travel across Africa or Australia, but the lush setting functions primarily as a metaphor for her tumultuous state. *Primitive, wild, savage* landscapes represent the sexuality she is trying to deal with. This use of geography is really racist. Of course the heroine never meets a black person to talk to! Not in romances written by white authors. What's at issue is simply her condition of husbandlessness. Her being *abroad* means that she lacks a home, a family, the Ideal Home that the perfect hero will provide for her. And, of course, this home is based on the model that the white middle class family is supposed to aspire to, even if the heroine ostensibly ends up in an eighteenth century palace in Venice or a nineteenth century cattle ranch in Texas.

CP: You could argue that both the modern and the medieval romance project an inner landscape on to the outside world. We gave ourselves permission to name it as a fantasy, whereas romance writers of your time are more obsessed with pretending the fantasy doesn't exist. But perhaps the difference isn't so great as you make out. Both sorts of romance are fundamentally about inner dramas, if you take the Jungian view. Which, I accept, is more concerned with essentials than with the different forms in which they historically occur.

MR: It still seems to me, Christine, that writers of your time were describing a wider world, that one of the purposes of the early romances was to sort out codes of behaviour that could ideally govern and define a community, not just a couple or a family. Modern romances are simply etiquette books on how to keep your man.

CP: But we too were describing, inventing I should perhaps say, a specific and limited world. An aristocratic one. A dream of aristocratic life. In that sense just like Barbara Cartland. It's true that we didn't always end with a happy marriage. *Tristan and Iseut*, for example, is about the disastrous consequences of adulterous love.

MR: At least you knew that romantic love was a pastime, a ritual, an art, a code. I wouldn't mind writing a romance that began from that position.

CP: So. Then tell me. Why would you want to write a romance? Since you've indicated that you agree with my saying that it's not possible for you to speak on behalf of other women, I think you'd better talk about what *you* feel.

MR: Let's see. Well, one thing that the medieval and the modern romance have in common is that they are often quest narratives. The medieval hero often goes off in search of the Holy Grail. The modern novel makes it possible for a woman to do this.

CP: To search for the Grail?

MR: For its modern equivalent. The lost mother. The Grail is the Good Breast. It sounds rather like a pub: at the Sign of the Good Breast. . . .

CP: But a minute ago you were saying that the modern heroine is only in quest of a husband. Now it turns out she wants her mother!

MR: The hero symbolizes the mother. He's actually not a man at all. I worked this out when I met Barbara Cartland. I was interviewing her for a magazine, and, to prepare myself, I read thirty or so of her novels. All of them ended with a paragraph describing a kiss: heavenly bliss; the sensation of transcendence. I became convinced that this wasn't just a euphemism for orgasm, but an image of the infant at the breast. Then I met Cartland herself. She *looked* like a breast: she was big and round and dressed in pink; she was swollen up like a meringue; she was a heap of sugar; she went on and on about honey. She fascinated me. Talking with her, I had the impression of someone who needed to be in complete control, who really needed a fantasy of omnipotence to compensate for all the tragedies in her personal life, who was extremely lonely in her power. Underneath the formidable charm of the millionairess bestseller, underneath the display of the power and wealth she so desperately needed to believe brought happiness, there was a little girl lost, a baby crying for her mother. Do I sound like a hack journalist? I *am* a hack journalist. Well, anyway, I started to see my own habit of voracious reading of novels, my need to tear into them and devour them, as my aggressive need for the absent maternal breast, my rage at its absence compensated for by the fantasies provided in the novels. On another level, the mother *is* lost in a patriarchal culture; I don't believe that little girls can get proper mothering in a world that is based on the power and status of fathers. Reading a novel compensates for two losses, two griefs: the loss of the actual breast every baby has regularly to experience; and the loss of the nurturing mother that little girls in particular experience. The loss of any symbol of the power of the female.

CP: The loss and the grief and the rage are so great that a woman might begin writing a novel, a romance, to convert the extreme pain of her suffering into something more bearable, something she could bear to feel inside herself?

MR: Yes. I think that's one of the roots of my own writing. And I might as well admit that I've got a strong drive towards writing romantic novels –

CP: Now we're getting there!

MR: – as well as a strong censoring drive that stops me from writing completely within the genre.

CP: Please explain what you mean. You use so much jargon and psychobabble when you talk; it quite baffles me.

MR: Well, although there's a move by certain feminist readers and critics to deny that the traditional romance is problematic for women, and to assert that reading it can be understood as a form of self-nurturance in the way I outlined just now, I find that inside me there's a terrific clash between my desires for writing about romantic bliss and my feminist ideas which are critical of this. I'd better explain what I mean about feminism. I'm not a feminist because I've suddenly seen the light about the oppression of women. I'm not a feminist because I've understood things that other women are too dumb to catch on to. I can't stand middle class feminists who pretend that feminism is a matter of simply using your brain, as though all women who aren't feminists are therefore stupid. I'm perfectly well aware that I became a feminist for reasons of class, to begin with: I was a middle class child growing up in the 1960s in a climate of economic growth and expansion. The world is yours, said my parents and teachers. I discovered it wasn't: it was a world for men. I was split in two: the woman, and the person who wanted to write. Feminism enabled me to articulate and explore this conflict. Subsequently I worked out that socialism was necessary for transforming the world into one women might want to live in. Being a socialist, a very critical, radical, feminist socialist, means accepting how privileged I am as a middle class person, as a white person. It means constantly having to explore all the clashing bits of me that make me feel quite mad a lot of the time; it means chucking out the humanist myth that says wholeness is possible (the humanist myth is only concerned, I think, with white middle class men), and it means writing about all this mess and muddle and conflict in me and trying to project it outside me into stories and characters. Er, please stop me if I am being boring.

CP: You're being a bit incoherent, but I think I catch your drift. Can you come to the point?

MR: The point is that my particular psychological history, my particular class position, my particular conflicts about femininity, make it difficult for me to imagine myself creating a heroine whose destiny could be summed up in the word *marriage* in the way that the traditional heroine of romance has her destiny summed up. But I also recognize in myself the drive to *avoid* exploring conflict, my own feelings of craziness and muddle; I catch myself writing, or wanting to write, about a woman achieving wholeness, being reunited with her mother, having nothing but wonderful sex with men, healing all the splits inside herself, and so on. These impulses are constantly subverted and challenged by their opposite. But just as I can't read only post-modernist anti-narrative texts all the time, because I also need to read stories and folktales and myths, so my writing comes out of two opposing tensions: the need to conceal, and the need to explore. I could never write a completely traditional romance, because my mad anti-humanist self would rise up and subvert it; I can't write only in an anti-narrative post-modernist way because that denies the romantic and religious part of me. Maybe I am just a bad writer.

CP: That is certainly something to think about. But before you retreat into orgies of self-pity, let's talk a bit more about the story that modern feminists might be telling in their versions of the romance. To what extent can the form be subverted?

MR: I'm not sure. I think it may be more a question of *relying* on aspects of the form that the reader will unconsciously recognize, thus providing her with the pleasure and desire necessary to stay with the text and keep on reading. A strong narrative seems fundamental for a start. Most people enjoy a story, a plot, wanting to discover what happens next. Secondly, it's a question of tailoring the myth of the lost mother to modern needs. A contemporary feminist author may not provide her heroine with a man. She may scorn such a substitute. She may give her main character a *woman* lover. The lost mother is triumphantly found through lesbian love. This is the direction that a whole generation of women's novels have taken. The heroine discovers her true self and sexuality through acknowledging her lesbianism. This is the first story that many women of my generation have needed to tell, I think, often using the confessional, autobiographical form. What interests me is what the *second* story is about. The wound to the psyche, the wound of the lost mother, is temporarily healed by writing a myth of true love

between women, but I think it subsequently bursts
open again. What happens then? Does the author repeat
the same story, more or less, under a different guise,
sticking to her wish to find maternal love and
nurturance? Or can she allow herself to step sideways,
to look at the matter from a different angle? For
example, there's a lot of discussion in the women's
movement at the moment, especially in America, of
lesbian sado-masochism. Many lesbians argue against
S-M on the grounds that it simply duplicates the
conventional power relations of heterosexuals and is
therefore reactionary as a practice between feminists.
End of discussion. The sado-masochists themselves
argue that feminist lesbian sex is so sanitized and
sentimental that it avoids true passion and the
exploration of power and domination. Now, to put the
argument in literary terms, a conventional lesbian
romance may be so concerned with establishing the
finding of the lost, good, nurturing mother that it can
make no space for the exploration of 'bad' feelings,
angry feelings, just as the conventional heterosexual
romance smoothes over all conflict between the man
and the woman. I'd love to read a lesbian romance
which tackled head-on the anger and rage that women
can feel for each other, the way in which the bad
mother can surface in a relationship, the way in which
women can exercise power over each other. This is one
direction the feminist romance could move in. I've not
heard *one* critic of lesbian sado-masochism argue that
what's at issue is women's feelings for the *mother*; the
analysis is always that the sadism is what *men* do to
women. Hence the need for vanilla sex in practice and
happy endings in books. I'd like to read a romance
about a lesbian sadist!
CP: Perhaps you should write it yourself?
MR: Perhaps I should. In order to do so I'd have to
tackle my own censoring mechanism. So far I've

written three novels to some extent influenced by the romance genre, even if they've also to some extent tried to subvert it. The books came out of my life. I wrote one novel about a woman becoming reunited with her mother and with her lesbian lover, at a time when these were issues for me. I wrote a second novel about a woman becoming reunited with the lost masculine part of herself, at a time when I was deeply involved with exploring male-female relationships again. I wrote a third novel about a woman becoming re-united with God, finding God within herself, God as an expression of the female, at a time when spirituality became important to me again. The search for wholeness, every time. And every novel supported by the feminist ideology of writing out of my own experience, allowing the problems in my own life to seek expression, and to some extent resolution, in novels. At the moment, since I've recently got married and now want to have a child, I'm writing a novel that takes off from questioning how a woman might be able to invent a marriage that suits her, how she imagines her way through to deciding she is able to become a mother. I'm writing in a much wilder and freer way than I've done for some time, and I'm allowing myself to tell and re-tell old myths, make things up. It feels good and liberating to give my imagination free rein. But I'm shy of writing a lesbian romance about sado-masochism, since I'm not actively involved in it myself at the moment. Here my feminist censor steps in waving a big stick and saying, No you can't do this, you can't tell another woman's story for her.

CP: That is absurd. Anyway I don't believe you. If you have written about lesbianism in the past, you can do so again. The lesbian in you is still alive and well, even if she expresses her love and desire for other women through passionate friendships rather than through, shall we say, specifically sexual relationships.

MR: Absolutely. That's correct. I haven't lost her, and don't want to.

CP: Similarly, the sado-masochist in you is alive and well also, if you have written novels about love affairs. You can't write honestly about love if you don't discuss power. You know all about your own capacities for sadism and for masochism.

MR: That's also true.

CP: So you could, if you wanted, really wanted to explore this area, give yourself permission to write about lesbian sado-masochism. Just grab the censor's stick and tell her to be off. She's another version of Virginia Woolf's angel in the house. These days the angel is a correct feminist.

MR: It would be interesting to try to do it. I should like to see how much anger and nastiness a romance could contain before it stopped being a romance and turned into something else. I should like to discover the boundary between pornography, the traditional home of descriptions of sado-masochism, and the romance, the traditional home of descriptions of love and nurturance. It's a cliché that romance represents for women what pornography represents for men. This distinction is based on woman as masochist and man as sadist. Whereas if I wrote about a woman sadist I'd be *joining* the romance genre to that of pornography, denying the traditional split between them.

CP: Yet another myth of wholeness surfaces!

MR: That *is* my myth: the quest for wholeness. Even though I criticize it, I'm fascinated by it. Jung argued that the image of God inside us, if it's to do us any good, needs to express our knowledge of both good and evil, that we shouldn't split the evil off and call it the devil but should own it. Most of us prefer to project evil away from us, on to others whom we then feel it is permissible to hate because they are so bad.

Similarly, in writing a romance, it could be important to join together, in my prose, the knowledge of the bad mother to the knowledge of the good mother. I often tend to write sentimentally about women and I've just understood why: it's because my quest for the good nurturing mother can take over so completely that I forget about her shadow side, her bad side. I've tended to write about the bad daughter and the good mother, or the yearning daughter rejected by the bad mother, but I've not let myself create a woman character who is both good *and* bad. Perhaps now I can let myself do so. Eureka!

CP: This is beginning to feel like a therapy session. Calm down.

MR: No, listen. Because I was so fed up with reading male fantasies of women, women characters invented by men in a stereotypical way, like Balzac's holy wives and mothers set against his corrupt courtesans for example, I started inventing women characters who were, for example, both mothers and lesbians, or both mothers and artists; but what I didn't see was that I was as much in the grip of *splits* as any male writer. My feminist desire for women to be seen as *good*, in my terms, got in the way of my honesty about what women are capable of.

CP: Well, I'm glad we've got that sorted out, at least. So, now you're ready to write a lesbian sado-masochist romantic pornographic epic. You've got a lot of work ahead of you. I think you'd better make a start. Whether your readers will see what you produce as a *romance* is another matter.

MR: Luckily that's up to them. They'll read it as they like.

CP: What I also wonder is whether the women who read romances, not just the feminist socialist critics and the middle class women who come out as fans of Georgette Heyer, will read this book of essays?

MR: I don't know. I somehow think not. It might depend on how much spare time they've got for reading, and whether they'd want to spend some of that precious time dissecting fantasies rather than simply enjoying having them. Perhaps it's only middle class women like me who can afford to sit around self-indulgently examining our psyches.

CP: Middle class guilt rearing its head. It's not helpful. You need to accept that there are *differences*, based on class and race, between women. Don't be patronizing. Perhaps you'd better include a discussion of feminist snobbery in your romance?

MR: Yes, all right. I think I'll set the opening scene in the hot garden of an old house in Italy. Two women are seated in the shade of a huge lavender bush, discussing their favourite romances. They look deeply into one another's eyes. Sweat courses down from their armpits. Crickets chirp. And one says to the other —

CP: — a spot of flagellation before or after dinner?

MR: Yes! And then —

CP: You'd better write it.

Index